THE FREE
DISRUPT OR DIE
COMPANION COURSE

DISRUPTORDIEBOOK.COM/STEP1

T O HELP GUIDE you through *Disrupt or Die*, I created a free Companion Course that you can get access to which includes downloadable checklists, bonus video content and links to resources mentioned in this book. This is your first step toward success with the content in this book, so I highly recommend you sign up now. Inside, the supplemental materials in this free course are organized by the sections and chapters of this book, making it easy for you to find what you need as you read along.

There's also an additional bonus section with content beyond what is shared here in the book, including more case studies and interviews to help you on your journey. I'll be adding more material in this bonus section over time, so make sure to visit the web address below and get free instant access to it now! See you on the inside!

Visit the following link to get free access to your Disrupt or Die bonus materials now:

DISRUPTORDIEBOOK.COM/STEP1

DISRUPT OR DIE

DISRUPT OR DIE

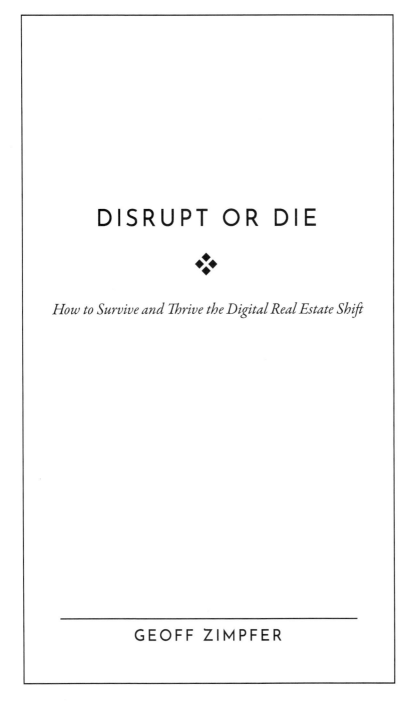

How to Survive and Thrive the Digital Real Estate Shift

GEOFF ZIMPFER

TABLE OF
CONTENTS

ACKNOWLEDGEMENTS

T HIS BOOK HAS been a labor of love, made possible by those who are leading by example in our industry, whose stories and encouragement helped bring this book to life.

Many mentors, both personal and indirect have shaped influenced me in writing this book. While there are too many names to list here, many of the guests interviewed on the Mortgage Marketing Radio podcast deserve recognition for their contributions. I am grateful for their eagerness to share their stories and help others.

There are a few people who have had significant impact and deserve special mention.

Tony Robbins for laying the foundation that changed to course of my life, Tom Ferry for the inspiration to expand my vision, Tim Braheem for his mastery of language, Barry Habib for leading the way with education, Todd Duncan for demonstrating how to build a professional mortgage practice, Dave Savage for arming us with the platform to help us differentiate and win, Bill Hart for his profound wisdom and Tim Davis for taking on chance on me, helping to grow my impact and influence within the real estate industry. I am grateful to you all.

Last but not least, I owe so much to my wife and family who allow me the space and time to create and whose encouragement kept me moving forward during the torturous process of writing a book.

COVID-19

I N LATE MARCH, this book was ready for publishing when
suddenly the world stopped.

The Coronavirus pandemic swept across the world, impacting the
global economy and our daily life.

I made the hard decision to pause publishing the book because,
frankly, I needed time process what was happening. It's been a
roller coaster ride for most of us. My primary hope is that you and
your family are healthy and you're maintaining an optimistic view
for your future.

As things unfolded over the past several weeks, I could see the
impact Covid-19 would have on consumers and the real estate
industry.

This book is written as a wake-up call for mortgage and real
estate professionals. Even before Covid-19, disruptive forces were
impacting your business and your future.

Many of the concepts and ideas within this book will happen
faster because of the pandemic. As we return to a "new normal"
certain less affected will return social gatherings and events. Others more hard hit by the virus will likely see a more cautious
approach.

For many Americans, the Coronavirus crisis calls to mind 9/11 or
the 2008 financial crisis—events that reshaped society in lasting

ways, from how we travel and buy homes, to the level of security and surveillance we're accustomed to, and our behaviors.

COVID-19 HAS RE-ORDERED VIRTUALLY EVERY INDUSTRY IN THE WORLD.

WE KNOW THAT touching things, being with other people and breathing the air in an enclosed space can be risky. How quickly that awareness recedes will be different for individuals, but it can never vanish completely for anyone who lived through this. It could become second nature to recoil from shaking hands or touching our faces—and we might all find we can't stop washing our hands.

The coronavirus pandemic is going to cause significant damage to business and lives. But it will force us to reconsider who we are and what we value, and, in the long run, it could help us rediscover the better version of ourselves.

When all is said and done, perhaps we will recognize their sacrifice as true patriotism, saluting our doctors and nurses, genuflecting and saying, "Thank you for your service," as we now do for military veterans.

This recovery cycle could look like a "V," or possibly more of a narrow "U," with a sharp drop but also a strong upswing, coming at some time in the second half of this year. There will be a return at some point of pent-up demand, from people who were unable during the lockdown to go out buy and return to a "new normal."

But crisis moments also present opportunity: more sophisticated and flexible use of technology, less polarization, a revived appreciation for the outdoors and life's other simple pleasures.

Instead of asking, "Is there a reason to do this online?" we'll be asking, "Is there any good reason to do this in person?"—and might need to be reminded and convinced that there is.

The paradox of online communication will be ratcheted up: It creates more distance, yes, but also more connection, as we communicate more often with people who are physically farther and farther away—and who feel safer to us because of that distance.

Closing delays are going to be the new normal during the COVID-19 pandemic. In a growing number of states, real estate contracts now contain a coronavirus addendum/amendment.

Sellers who are interested in a quick real estate deal through an *iBuyer*, like Opendoor or Zillow Offers, will have to wait. Both Opendoor and Zillow Offers, as well as similar firms, have paused transactions. This reduces the chances that iBuyer employees are exposed to COVID-19, and it also reduces the chances of mass attempts to liquidate homes for cash in a financial panic.

The future if iBuyers is on hold – for the moment. For more details, iBuyers are discussed in Chapter Five of this book.

In a *survey* of more than 3,000 Realtors conducted March 16-17 by the National Association of Realtors, 48% reported a decrease in homebuyer interest due to the Coronavirus outbreak.

The effects on real estate will vary by sector and market, and the extent of the effects will depend upon the duration of the economic shutdown and return to healthy unemployment levels.

WHAT CONSUMERS WANT

REAL ESTATE IS changing faster because of COVID-19. Agents and lenders all across the country and forced to rethink almost every aspect of their business — closing deals remotely, integrating technology, how you show up online and prioritizing service over sales.

There was a housing shortage before the virus. There will be even less inventory during and after the shutdown as more people hit the pause button.

Consumers will do far more virtual tours of homes and will not waste time visiting homes that do not meet the criteria. So rather than visiting 10 homes physically in person, consumers would likely have narrowed their in person visits to only two homes.

Consumers will be open to meeting via Zoom for buyer consultations, pre-approvals, and inspection report reviews.

For now, buying real estate sight-unseen may feel uncomfortable for most buyers to consider. But Covid-19 has shifted consumer behavior and expectations.

The technology to deliver high-resolution, interactive 3-D virtual reality, so buyers will feel like they're walking through the property in person; exists today.

And not just the way the house looked when it was mapped. Increasingly, virtual reality tours will allow viewers to see the natural light at different times of day and even different times of the year.

Buyers won't even have to use their imagination to determine how their furniture will look in it. Virtual reality software like BoxBrownie.com will let them superimpose various pieces of furniture in the space.

Prospective buyers will be able to virtually walk through dozens of homes in an afternoon from the comfort of their own home, with these virtual tours available through their agent – YOU!

A recent Realtor.com *survey* revealed that with access to accurate listing data, detailed photos, virtual and live video tours, 24% of people would be willing to buy a home without seeing it in person and 30% would be willing to rent one. Further, 21% of people agree that COVID-19 has made them more likely to move into a home sight unseen.

When asked to select which technology features would be most helpful when deciding on a new home, responses in order of preference were:

1. A virtual tour of the home (61 percent)

2. Accurate and detailed listing information (58 percent)

3. Accurate and detailed neighborhood information (53 percent)

4. High quality listing photos (51 percent)

5. The ability for my agent or landlord to walk me through the property via video chat (39 percent)

SELLERS ARE WARY OF OPEN HOUSES BUT OPEN TO LISTING PHOTOS AND VIRTUAL TOURS.

WHEN ASKED ABOUT selling a home within the next six months, respondents showed a slight discomfort toward holding open houses, but were still generally open to allowing their agent and some shoppers inside. Potential sellers are most comfortable with:

1. Allowing their agent in the home to take photos (56 percent)

2. Allowing their agent in the home to give a virtual tour (55 percent)

3. Having an agent walk a buyer through the home in person (47 percent)

4. Having an agent walk a buyer through the home via video chat (44 percent)

5. Holding an open house (35 percent)

Transitioning into the digital world is more important now than ever. Are you preparing for the "new normal?"

YOUR OPPORTUNITY

NOW IS THE time to pivot your business, show up and be of service. Smart agents and lenders are stepping up their presence on social media with relevant content, helping people make sense of the housing and mortgage markets for your local area.

The same marketing message of "now's a great time to buy/sell" or "low rates/fast closing" are not the right narrative for the current situation.

How do you show up? By first getting yourself educated to share content that provides context, so people feel confident to make a decision.

Are you innovating and adapting to overcome? Do you know how the housing market has performed in previous recessions? Are you showing up online with relevant data?

Get yourself educated with your FREE COMPANION COURSE included with this book.

Your first module is: YOUR NEXT 90 DAYS HOW TO PREPARE YOUR BUSINESS FOR AFTER CORONAVIRUS

Visit the following link to get free access to your Disrupt or Die bonus materials now:

DISRUPTORDIEBOOK.COM/STEP1

THREE THINGS YOU CAN DO RIGHT NOW:

1) Create a "As Soon as This Passes" Plan

Let's be totally clear about something: THIS SEASON OF ANXI-ETY AND SOCIAL DISTANCING WILL PASS. We're going to figure this thing out, and life (and your real estate business) are going to start making moves back to normal. Sometimes it's hard for your clients to see past their current fears, so help them do that with a personalized "as soon as this passes" plan over a Zoom call.

2) Make Five Calls, Send Five Texts, Write Five Thank You Cards

Don't let this time of social distancing be a time of community isolation.

Set aside some time each day to make five phone calls to your sphere. Talk to them about what's going on in their lives, tell them about your new normal, and if it comes up, chat about the real estate market.

Likewise, shoot off five text messages to people you know, letting them know that you're thinking of them and that you hope they're well. This sort of empathetic outreach spurs conversation and creates a connection that you can build on.

Finally, find five people that you can thank with a personalized, hand-written card. It can make a world of difference for someone, and in this challenging time, a little encouragement is a great idea.

3) Organize Your CRM

If used properly, your CRM tracks every client interaction, helps you identify lead opportunities, and gives you the tools to manage your lead funnel so that the most important clients get the attention they need at the time they need it.

A CRM's effectiveness is magnified when your clients' profiles are filled out with as much information as possible. A name, phone number, and email address are great, but imagine the sort of personalized, timely communication you could plan for your clients if you had birthdays, anniversaries, closing dates, and social media profiles there?

Go through each of your contacts one by one, find and fill in as much information as you can.

THE GOOD NEWS

MAJOR FINANCIAL INSTITUTIONS including Goldman Sachs and JP Morgan are calling for a 'V' shaped recovery with a return to positive GDP in Q3 and Q4.

Home appreciation forecasts from Zelman and Associates for post Covid-19 show positive appreciation growth range of ~ 4%.

There are motivated buyers and sellers active *right now* and even more waiting in the wings. Get with your lender, collaborate on buyer consultations over Zoom.

With every transaction, real estate in America touches 13 jobs. It represents 5% of our GDP.

YOU can play a role in the story of housing leading us out of the current economic situation.

Get yourself educated with your FREE COMPANION COURSE included with this book.

Your first module is: YOUR NEXT 90 DAYS HOW TO PREPARE YOUR BUSINESS FOR AFTER CORONAVIRUS

Visit the following link to get free access to your Disrupt or Die bonus materials now:

DISRUPTORDIEBOOK.COM/STEP1

PREFACE

W HEN I ENTERED the real estate industry in 2003, I fell in love.

In love with the people I had the privilege of serving to help them purchase a home, with the real estate professionals, colleagues and affiliates who became strategic partners and some who even became close friends. You could say I found "my calling."

This book came to life because as I traveled North America speaking with hundreds of real estate and mortgage professionals, I noticed a recurring theme in our conversations.

There was a lot of noise, confusion and even fear regarding the impact of technology and the future of our roles in real estate. Business had been done a certain way for decades and many weren't prepared for the changes arising from digital shift.

Some lacked the confidence to embrace new mediums of communication while most were simply confused and overwhelmed on what to do.

Through hundreds of interviews, hours of research and personal application in my own business, I discovered some interesting truths. There are no secrets. The principles of sales and marketing haven't really changed. Yes, there are new tactics and tools however, "old school" marketing is alive and well. Consumers still crave human interaction and value the guidance of competent real estate and mortgage professionals.

What I'm offering you in this book is a high-level, truthful discussion about our current and future business realities, distilled from reliable research, real case studies and expert opinions.

There is no one-size-fits-all marketing solution. I'm not going to tell you what to do ... or not to do. Use this book as your guide. You'll have to make your own decisions about the best paths for your own unique situation and how you'll get there.

AND OH, BY THE WAY, THERE ARE FREE GIFTS!

I've created a free *Disrupt or Die Companion Course* with checklists, bonus videos and resources to help guide you even further along your journey. To get free access to the Companion Course, which I do recommend you do use while you read this book, go to: DISRUPTORDIEBOOK.COM/COURSE

Let's get started!

PART I:
FIVE TRENDS DRIVING THE DIGITAL REAL ESTATE SHIFT

T HE ADVENT OF technology has called into question the future role of real estate agents and mortgage loan originators. Well funded tech firms are attempting to disrupt and relegate the role of agent and lender in similar fashion to the once prominent travel agent.

People are more comfortable than ever integrating technology into all aspects of their lives and demand efficiency, speed and personalization. If you're going to survive the digital shift, you have to start with understanding how we arrived here.

In Part I, we'll look at the evolution of technology, and trends driving consumer behavior.

CHAPTER 1:
THE RISE OF THE
DIGITAL CULTURE

A DECADE AGO, smartphones (as we know them by today's standards) didn't exist. Three decades earlier, no one even owned a computer. Think about that—the first personal computers arrived about 40 years ago.

Computer chips have become increasingly powerful while costing less. This is because, over the last five decades, the number of transistors—or the tiny electrical components that perform basic operations—on a single chip have been doubling regularly.

This exponential doubling, known as Moore's Law, is the reason a modern smartphone affordably packs so much dizzying capability into such a small package.

American author, inventor, and futurist, Ray Kurzweil, wrote in 2001 that every decade our overall rate of progress was doubling. According to Kurzweil, "We won't experience 100 years of progress in the 21st century—it will be more like 20,000 years of progress (at today's rate)."

In 1990, he predicted that a computer would beat a pro chess player by 1998; this became true in 1997, when Garry Kasparov lost to IBM's Deep Blue. In 2016, a computer mastered the even more complex game Go—an accomplishment not expected by some experts for another decade.

The graphic below represents the evolution of technology and its continued integration and acceptance into our daily lives.

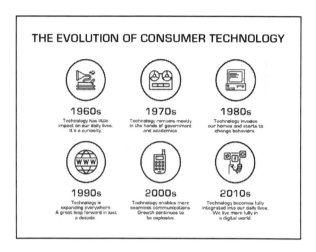

The progress has been pretty stunning—the global adoption of the Internet, smartphones, ever-more agile robots, AI that learns.

REMEMBER "GOING TO THE BANK?"

IT'S HARD TO imagine there was once a time when all banking was conducted at actual brick-and-mortar financial institutions. Today, you can check your account balance, send money, withdraw cash, transfer funds and more—right from your smartphone.

REMEMBER WHEN AMAZON SOLD ONLY BOOKS?

WHEN JEFF BEZOS launched Amazon.com in 1994, he gave himself a 30% chance of success—slightly better than the 1 in 10 odds for Internet start-ups. But two decades after its launch, Amazon has conquered ecommerce, racking up total revenues of $280 billion in 2019.

THE INTERNET OF THINGS (IOT)

THE INTERNET OF Things, or IoT, refers to the billions of physical devices around the world that are now connected to the internet, collecting and sharing data. For consumers, the smart home is probably where they are likely to come into contact with internet-enabled things, and it's one area where the big tech companies (in particular Amazon, Google, and Apple) are competing hard.

The most obvious of these are smart speakers, such as Amazon's Echo, but there are also smart plugs, lightbulbs, cameras, thermostats, and the much-mocked smart fridge. Depending on the features built into the fridge, it lets you look at a calendar, look up recipes, watch TV, play music, send and receive pictures, and leave notes. LG is also developing a smart refrigerator with a built-in display that will let you order groceries.

"ALEXA...IS VOICE IS THE NEW SEARCH?"

THE ECHO DOT ranked among the best-selling products on all of Amazon during Black Friday and Cyber Monday.

In this ever-emerging field of technology, voice search is the newest trend in tech. Just as users got used to mobile devices instead of home phones, text messages as the new email, and social media as the new word-of-mouth, it is likely that voice search will eventually become the same after some time.

It is no surprise that most smart speakers are used at home while voice search on mobile devices are more likely to be used in the car. Currently, Amazon is releasing a new Alexa product for your car to assist with commands like navigation and voice to text.

In fact, according to comScore, 50% of all searches will be done by voice by 2020, and 30% of searches will be done without even a screen, according to Gartner. As voice becomes a part of things we use every day in our cars, phones and even our homes, it will become the new "norm."

Amazon CTO Werner Vogels stated "what voice will do is allow you to have a normal, natural way of communicating; voice is the key disruption."

REMEMBER A WORLD BEFORE UBER?

IN 1997, WE were warned not to talk to strangers on the internet, much less get into cars with them at night or in unfamiliar places. In 2020, we use the internet to bring strangers to our homes, businesses, and wherever we happen to be—and get in their cars.

At the swipe of a finger and tap of a button, you can hail a car through your smartphone. Within minutes, you are picked up at your desired location and whisked off to your final destination, whether it's the grocery store, movie theater, airport or the hottest restaurant in town.

Uber's official newsroom reports that over Uber's nearly 10 years of operation, 5 billion trips have been completed worldwide. This figure is climbing rapidly, with 15 million Uber trips completed each day.

Uber's nearest competitor, Lyft, has enjoyed a few years of healthy growth, taking market share away from Uber. Like Uber, Lyft is conducting experiments with self-driving cars.

By mid-2019, over $1 billion had been invested in at least twenty-five different flying car companies. A dozen vehicles are currently being test-flown. Uber and Hyundai unveiled a flying taxi at the Consumer Electronics show in Las Vegas that may eventually transform your ridesharing trips.

The first actual prototype will be ready in 2023, according to a Hyundai spokesperson. A human pilot will fly the air taxi until the companies finalize software to autonomously control it, the company said.

"It's going to be a while," said William Crossley, a Purdue University professor who researches aerospace design. "If things go well, it's certainly plausible in the next 10 years."

HOUSING INDUSTRY

TECHNOLOGY IS A bit behind the trend in the housing industry, but this is all beginning to change.

HousingWire's Tech100 Award recognizes companies offering the most innovative technology solutions for the U.S. housing industry. To inform readers on the some of the biggest tech trends today and where housing tech will be five years into the future, HousingWire asked SparkTank Media Founder and CEO Jeff Lobb—where do you see real estate tech in five years?

- The standard open house will be mainly virtual in the initial shopping experience.

- Technology will make appointments for you and open doors remotely.

- An interested passerby of a home for sale will have access to that data on demand due to its geo location.

- Listings will notify buyers instead of agents having to send it to them.

THE RISE OF BLOCKCHAIN

DISRUPTIVE TECHNOLOGIES LIKE blockchain have the potential to transform and replace expensive processes such as title search and title transfer. What is blockchain? Here's a useful definition:

> A blockchain is a decentralized, distributed and public digital ledger that is used to record transactions across many computers so that any involved record cannot be altered retroactively, without the alteration of all subsequent blocks.

Boy that's clear isn't it? The thing to know is that blockchain technology may radically alter the process through which consumers buy a home, as well as the way financial institutions handle mortgages.

Specifically, blockchain could remove cost and friction from the real estate sales process, create transaction records that are infallible and incorruptible, and facilitate near-instantaneous settlements.

Companies like Homelend are going all-in on technology-based solutions that revolve around blockchain. The company connects lenders and borrowers directly, removing many of the steps involved in the process—legal, underwriting, and more—and replaces them with artificial intelligence and machine learning technology. The length of the pre-qualification and approval process can be cut by nearly half.

Over time, what you could see, for example, is a mortgage being granted in 10 minutes. You could see a letter of credit being granted in two minutes.

It is not unthinkable that one day in the near future the entire mortgage underwriting and approval process will be seamlessly enabled by technology without a single human touch point.

These blockchain-based solutions have real potential for disruption and could eliminate many of the process related inefficiencies that plague the mortgage industry. However, the tools are still in their relative infancy, and their adoption remains the largest concern.

CONSUMERS WANT A BETTER MORTGAGE EXPERIENCE

UNTIL RECENTLY, THE mortgage process has seen little change from the process 20 or 30 years ago—slow, inefficient, complicated, a mountain of paperwork and requiring manual intervention at every step from application and processing, to underwriting and closing.

Plus, it's been a daunting experience—especially for first-time buyers. The amount of personal information required feels invasive and repetitive. With so many moving parts and parties involved, not to mention a ticking clock, the mortgage process is not something consumers have looked forward to.

Currently, the average cost to originate a mortgage is close to $9,000 per loan, according to the Mortgage Bankers Association.[1] Many disparate systems and manual labor are the key reasons for such high cost. Automating many of those manual tasks, the cost would drop significantly.

Why does it take so long to process a mortgage? According to loan software company Ellie Mae, it takes an average of 43 days to close a home purchase loan as of June 2019.[2] Digital processing should be able to reduce the turnaround time from origination to completion dramatically—from months to days, and eventually hours.

And third, why can't consumers get the process started any time they want? The desire for a mortgage does not limit itself to business hours. Consumers want what they want when they want it.

---

1. http://bit.ly/39gSxVt
2. http://bit.ly/2UuMpEU

That means 24/7 access to service, with or without human intervention, and on any medium, with as little data input as possible.

Of course, there are companies already offering applications online. You can apply for a mortgage on your computer or phone, and that's the first step in the right direction.

Consumers want speed, price and convenience. But consumers also want a professional, knowledgable person to talk to when things go wrong, or to provide personal advice for their specific situation.

> In 2019, 88% of all homebuyers and 98 percent of homebuyers aged 37 and youner financed their home purchase.
>
> **National Association of REALTORS®**

Having a professional, knowledgeable, friendly guide during the home-buying and selling journey will likely be the best balance of old and new to make the digital future of real estate an inviting place to do business.

WILL MACHINES EVENTUALLY REPLACE HUMANS?

SOME BELIEVE ARTIFICIAL intelligence will disrupt the human interaction with homebuyers and remove loan officers entirely from the equation. However, data does not suggest this will happen anytime soon. According to consumer research by Pricewaterhouse Coopers, today's borrowers prefer a combination of digital tools with knowledgeable advisors.[3]

---

3. https://pwc.to/36ZbAln

It might thin the crowd, but it won't completely replace the need for human interaction during an emotional process like buying a home. Not in our lifetime.

There is still too much emotion and uncertainty involved in the home buying or selling process. We raise families in homes, our lives are centered around homes. There is emotion tied with dozens of moving parts during the buying and selling process that a human with experience in the field is absolutely a valuable asset.

Will mortgage professionals need to adapt to new tech and pivot with their value proposition? To remain relevant and win the attention of modern consumers; yes, indeed.

TECHNOLOGY SOLVES PROBLEMS

TECHNOLOGY IS THE reflection of people's imagination on solving existing problems. These problems push human beings to transform their imagined ideas to solving these problems into technological innovations which, as a result, improve life.

From Digital assistants like Alexa and Google Assistant, to having thermostats and garage doors controlled by an iPhone, to the technology that allows smart locks to open with a remote device or with a user's thumbprint, smart tech adds a level of convenience we have never had before.

Furthermore, as a technology becomes more effective, it attracts more attention. The result is a flood of new resources—such as increased investment in technologies, people and companies—which are directed to further improving the technology and solving problems.

The future is approaching much faster than we realize. It's critical to think exponentially about where we're headed, how you can be prepared and understand how you can profit from technology vs. be disrupted and displaced.

In Part II, we'll provide a framework with examples on how to become a modern, mortgage or real estate professional and "disrupt proof" your career.

CHAPTER 2:
THE RISE OF
CONSUMER CONTROL

T HE INTERNET HAS significantly changed the home buying and selling experience. Remember the good old days when Real Estate Agents used to be the gatekeepers?

Before the rise of technology, searching and finding homes online, each agent was issued a large "listing book" every two weeks. Often, the information was obsolete by the time the books were printed and delivered.

Each book was clearly marked "Confidential" on the cover, and the information inside was unobtainable directly by the public. Agents were the gatekeepers of the sacred scrolls and were paid well to dispense the information as the need arose.

Today, all that information and much, much more is freely available to anyone with a smartphone.

It might seem as if technology is not only allowing consumers to conduct the business of real estate with increasing convenience and efficiency but is also lessening the reliance on real estate professionals.

With new technologies like Toor, deemed "the world's smartest lockbox," and ZipTours you can schedule showings, show up to a home without an Agent present and even have an agent streamed live to your phone to ask questions or make offers.

Now, before you panic, unrepresented buyers have to register and request showings ahead of time. Sellers and Listing Agents can deny the showing, if desired. In addition, Toor has partnered with an identification verification company to help ensure the safety of property, customers, and Agents.

You might come to the conclusion that a real estate agent is no longer considered a necessary part of the buying or selling process. However, the opposite seems to be the case. With more and more people finding their perfect homes online, they're looking to their agent and lender to act as an advisor who can help them through the buying process.

According to Bob Goldberg, CEO of the National Association of REALTOR's, typical real estate transactions now involve as many as 200 complicated steps or procedures —many of which happen in the period between contract and close, such as navigating the loan process, arranging home inspections and managing paperwork

Data from the 2019 NAR Profile of Homebuyers and Sellers Report shows that 89% of all buyers and sellers engaged the services a real estate agent or broker.[1]

CONSUMERS DON'T WANT TO FIND AND ANALYZE ALL THAT DATA

I BELIEVE THE reason for consumers continuing to work with real estate professionals is clear. Yes, finding and reading information about homes for sale is easier now that it has ever been. Buyers don't need an Agent to do that.

However, understanding, interpreting, and applying that information is not so easy. If you've never bought a home before or

---

1. http://bit.ly/2SATtof

even if the last home you bought was several years ago, you can easily drown in today's mad dash between contract and closing.

Today's home loan applicant faces multiple pitfalls on the road to a successful closing.

Appraisals come in low, inspections come back with nitpicky issues, lenders demand more documentation and buyers want to feel they are making the right choice for their situation with professional guidance.

Agents, once the gatekeepers of listings, are adapting to a world in which people can easily browse all the properties they want. With increased control, consumers have ubiquitous access to information, forcing agents and loan originators to adjust their value proposition.

Even though there is a lot of data on the Internet, homebuyers don't want to spend hours and hours trying to find it, read it, analyze it, and understand it. They would rather agents and lenders do it for them.

This is where today's agents and a competent lender demonstrate their ability to engineer a real estate transaction. That's why nine out of ten home sellers were assisted by a Real Estate Agent or Broker last year.

According to Fannie Mae's 2019 National Housing Survey,[2] fewer people are using their lender as a primary source for information. Just 47% now compared with 58% in 2015. Now people are using websites instead to self-educate.

Is your website a source of education for prospects?

Ryan Grant is consistently ranked among the top 100 Mortgage Originators in the nation. His team has developed a platform

---

2. http://bit.ly/2Hozr9P

called "The Art of Home Ownership", which consists of several unique ways that the consumer will benefit from being their client before, during, and after the transaction.

With the platform, Grant's team takes a proactive stance in educating borrowers to grow their wealth and make smart decisions about real estate and finance. Rather than just quoting rates and closing loans, his team's job is to remove the fear, anxiety, and uncertainty that the majority of consumers have, and replace it with excitement, confidence and motivation.

The business of real estate has shifted from being a provider of information, to *assisting* consumers in understanding the overwhelming barrage of information by providing meaningful interpretation and implementation of a personalized solution.

How about you? Have you made the shift from quoting rates, fees and features to leading with education and guidance?

CHAPTER 3:
THE RISE OF MOBILE

I N CASE YOU hadn't already noticed, mobile devices are now most people's preferred way to access the Internet and its vast content. That's partially because smartphone adoption continues to rise (nearly 80% of Americans own one), and the average user is now spending more than three hours per day on their phones.

MOBILE STATS (SOURCE: STATISTA)

- IN 2019, 52% OF ALL WEBSITE TRAFFIC WORLDWIDE WAS GENERATED THROUGH MOBILE PHONES

- GOOGLE DRIVES 95% OF ALL US PAID SEARCH AD CLICKS ON MOBILE

- 93% OF FACEBOOK'S ADVERTISING REVENUE COMES FROM MOBILE

- 80% OF SOCIAL MEDIA TIME IS SPENT ON A MOBILE DEVICE

- MORE THAN 50% OF VIDEOS ARE WATCHED ON MOBILE

- WORLDWIDE, MORE PEOPLE OWN A CELL PHONE THAN A TOOTHBRUSH

It's hard to believe that it has been less than a decade since Apple and Google opened their own app stores.

Mobile apps have fundamentally transformed nearly every aspect of our lives-from ordering food to making a grocery list, checking account balances, and communicating with others...like the commercial said, "There's an app for that!"

Technology has improved and streamlined our day-to-day activities, disrupting the status quo and making things easier.

WHAT DROVE THE EXPLOSION IN POPULARITY OF MOBILE APPS?

THERE WERE TWO key factors that drove the massive growth of mobile apps:

1. Users loved the convenience of apps they could download and use on their phones.
2. Users carry their phones with them wherever they go. Together, these factors drove the expansion of mobile apps in ways desktop application developers couldn't envision.

Today's technologies are leveraging the magic of mobile apps by using them to manage the IoT (Internet of Things) networks in smart homes, empowering customers to manage their home's lighting, temperature, and electrical consumption from any location with a cell phone signal.

Automotive manufacturers have created apps that allow you to pair your phone with your car so you can remotely start it, find it in a parking lot, and even park it .

APPS HAVE TRANSFORMED OUR LIVES

FOR BETTER OR worse, social media apps have fundamentally influenced how we interact with each other. Through social media, we are able to easily interact with people from all over the world from our handheld mobile device.

Fitbit helps keep users in shape, Siri gives us directions when looking for sushi in a new city, and Amazon.com lets us order virtually anything we can think of with our phones.

We hail rides and order all the ingredients for dinner, tapping our phone against another to share a tasty recipe. From monitoring heartbeats to finding our dream home and navigating unknown streets, mobile apps enhance and extend our capabilities every day.

The rise of mobile use has also impacted consumer expectations for fast, convenient, and simple to use services. When it comes to buying, selling, or renovating a home, prospective homeowners are increasingly demanding the capability to have all pertinent data available or easily accessible from their mobile phone.

According to NAR's 2019 Home Buyer and Seller Generational Trends study, 76 PERCENT OF ALL BUYERS FOUND THEIR HOME ON A MOBILE DEVICE.[1]

---

1. http://bit.ly/2SATtof

> "The phone is by far the most important piece of technology in real estate. Deals get done on it. Contracts get created and sent on it. Homes get found on it. Marketing gets consumed on it. The old school phone with its new school capabilities will have a bigger impact on an agents bottom line for the next 5 years than all of the buzzwords (Blockchain, A.I., machine learning) combined."
>
> Chris Smith
> Co-Founder,Curaytor

THE FUTURE OF MOBILE

MOBILE CONTINUES TO disrupt traditional ways of getting things done. Advances in other technologies such as data storage and blockchain will drive innovation that transforms areas as diverse as finance and healthcare—all accessible from our mobile phone.

You need to understand the power of mobile. We, as a society, have personalized and prioritized mobile tech. These devices have become more important, perhaps, than any other technology- greater than radio, television, computers, and maybe even our cars.

According to Google's Micro-moments study, 87% of people always have their smartphone at their side, day and night.[2] On average, smartphone users check their phones 150 times per day, and 67 percent of smartphone users say they check their phones within 15 minutes of waking up.

We are often so obsessed with mobile devices that we've had to

---

2. http://bit.ly/2S13fJI

create laws to protect ourselves from misusing them. Distracted driving laws have been created in at least 46 states, banning text messaging while driving.

It's estimated that the average US adult will spend nearly 1 out of every 3 media minutes (30.6%) on a mobile device in 2019—up from less than 24% just four years ago. (eMarketer)[3]

After analyzing 900,000 mobile ads' landing pages spanning 126 countries, Google came to the conclusion that "the majority of mobile sites are slow and bloated with too many elements."

So what's the lesson?

Consumers expect businesses to provide them with media they can access on their mobiles devices, and Comscore reports that 57 percent of consumers wouldn't recommend a business whose mobile site experience has poor design.[4]

If you're not already investing in a MOBILE FIRST web presence and customer experience, to deliver a better client experience and streamline your business, you're behind the curve.

---

3. http://bit.ly/3biB3tC
4. http://bit.ly/39eDA6g

CHAPTER 4:
THE RISE OF SOCIAL MEDIA

A CCORDING TO ESTIMATES, the number of worldwide social media users has reached 3 billion people and is expected to continue to grow. Statista reports the number of social media users in the United States is projected to increase from 246 million to over 257 million users by 2023.

What's more, Statista reports the daily time spent on social media in the U.S is an average of 1 hour and 57 minutes with most of it happening on the most popular social platforms including Facebook, Instagram, YouTube and messaging apps like Whats App and Facebook Messenger.[1]

Today, we use social media to keep in touch with family and friends, dating, and sharing our personal experiences with the world. Social media, as a whole, is still growing with no end in sight.

The average homebuyer spends nearly 14 hours a week on social, and 65% say they are influenced by online friends' home-buying posts. After seeing that their online friends bought a home, about 33% of millennial first-time homebuyers say they reflect on their ability to do the same. (USA Today)[2]

That means that it's important for you to cultivate a strong social

---

1. http://bit.ly/3bfRNSf
2. http://bit.ly/2GXpFoY

media presence to remain relevant and bring in new referrals and leads.

THE TOP SOCIAL MEDIA SITES FOR YOUR BUSINESS

LET'S TAKE A look at the main sites most relevant for you as a mortgage or real estate professional.

FACEBOOK

ON A GLOBAL level, the market leader is Facebook, the first social media platform to surpass 1 billion registered accounts on both its desktop and mobile versions. As of September 2019, Facebook reports 2.45 billion active monthly users.

Facebook also leads the U.S. market, accounting for about 42 percent of all social media site visits in the country. Every 60 seconds on Facebook: 519,000 comments are posted, 317,000 statuses are updated, and 147,000 photos are uploaded. (Source: Omnicore)[3]

Of those who use Facebook, 74% of them log in daily. In fact, half of them actually check Facebook several times a day, spending an average of 35 minutes per day on the platform. (Source: Sprout Social)

It's easy to get started on Facebook, because almost all content formats work on Facebook. Text, images, videos, live videos, and stories.

However, the Facebook algorithm prioritizes video content over images and text. According to BuzzSumo, video posts are outperforming image posts by a whopping 73%![4]

---

3. http://bit.ly/2v8AK4o
4. http://bit.ly/2uncXgs

Facebook's mission was previously focused on "connecting the world." Today Facebook is about "giving people power to build community and bring the world closer together."

Leveraging Facebook's advertising capabilities to reach potential home-buyers and sellers can play a significant role in building your brand, generating leads and growing your business. We'll talk more about that in Chapter 8: Lead Generation.

YOUTUBE

YOUTUBE (OWNED BY Google) is the second largest search engine after Google. YouTube stated their 1.9 billion users spend an average of 1 hour a day watching videos on their mobile devices in 2019.

Even if it is not a traditional social media platform—it is now used by nearly three-quarters of U.S. adults and 94% of 18-to 24-year-olds. (Source: Pew Research Center)[5]

YouTube reports that its users watch a billion hours of videos every day and four hundred hours of video are uploaded to YouTube every minute.

In an average month, 8 out of 10 18-49 year-olds watch YouTube, and the time people spend watching YouTube on their TV has more than doubled in the last year.

If you are an agent or lender who is trying to decide if online video is a good way to reach your audience, these YouTube stats should demonstrate the amazing reach that can be had on YouTube.

If you want your personal brand to be on YouTube, in Chapter 6:

5. https://pewrsr.ch/2UuCWNN

The Brand Called You; you'll see how agents and lenders are succeeding with YouTube.

INSTAGRAM

INSTAGRAM IS A photo and video sharing social media app. It allows you to share a wide range of content such as photos, videos, Stories, and live videos. It has also recently launched InstagramTV (IGTV) for live and longer-form videos.

The app, which Facebook acquired for $1 billion in 2012, should generate $8 billion to $9 billion in revenue in 2019, depending on whose estimate you use.

Instagram reports there are over 1 billion Instagrammers—more than 700 million of whom use Instagram every single day, sharing an average of 95 million photos and videos per day.

Over 100 million Instagram users are from within the U.S; according to Omnicore, 43% of American women and 31% of men are active users.[6]

As a brand, you can have an Instagram business profile, which will provide you with rich analytics such as visitor traffic, clicks, user demographics and the ability to run ads to increase your personal brand exposure to generate leads.

Want to connect with first time homebuyers?

More than half of U.S. Millennials are active on Instagram, according to marketing research firm, eMarketer.

Instagram's momentum shows no signs of stopping, constantly pumping out new features. As its user base continues to expand its no longer just trendy—it's the most innovative, established

---

6. http://bit.ly/2v8s5yn

social network out there right now to get your listings and personal brand noticed.

LINKEDIN

LINKEDIN IS NOW more than just a resume and job search site. It has evolved into a professional social media site where industry experts share content, network with one another, and build their personal brand. It has also become a place for businesses to establish their thought leadership and authority in their industry and attract talent to their company.

The mission of LinkedIn is simple: connect the world's professionals to make them more productive and successful.

LinkedIn is the world's largest professional network with more than 575 million users in more than 200 countries and territories worldwide. In December 2016, Microsoft completed its $26.2 billion acquisition of LinkedIn.

LinkedIn users use the platform for a variety of reasons, including networking, finding best practices or advice on things relatable to their career, etc. LinkedIn is a powerful tool that can be used for facilitating groups where like-minded people can come together and collaborate. You can ask questions, respond to issues and comments, and finally post information or articles that are helpful.

LinkedIn also offers advertising opportunities, such as boosting your content, sending personalized ads to LinkedIn inboxes, and displaying ads by the side of the site. Currently, the cost of LinkedIn ads, compared to advertising on other social networks, is comparatively high.

Marketing Agency Omnicore reports there are 56% of male users and 44% female users on LinkedIn with 25% of Millennials using LinkedIn.[7] Think your first time homebuyers aren't on LinkedIn?

There are 87 million Millennials on LinkedIn with 11 million in decision-making positions.

44% of Linked users earn more than $75,000 in a year and 91% of marketing executives list LinkedIn as the top place to find quality content.

Nearly 60% of LinkedIn users access the network from their phones, so prime your posts for mobile viewing. Keep your posts short, and make them compelling with interesting imagery and video.

LINKEDIN VIDEO

LINKEDIN INTRODUCED NATIVE video functionality last year so users can now film or upload video directly to LinkedIn using the LinkedIn app on their phones or via the website on their desktop computer.

Wordstream reported that 59% of executives prefer video over text, another reason why LinkedIn now offers native video on its platform.[8]

Once you post a video, you get access to the same audience insights you see with all your other LinkedIn posts. Discover the titles and locations of your viewers, where they work, and view engagement stats like total views, likes, and comments.

Now you'll know exactly how well your video content is performing on LinkedIn, since you'll see insights directly from the app.

Building your audience on LinkedIn for mortgage and real estate professionals is the same as it is for any other industry. Once you optimize your LinkedIn profile, start building your network

7. http://bit.ly/31xzAuX
8. http://bit.ly/2S1IsG6

through existing contact lists, professional groups, and your website.

While there may be more people and activity on other social media sites, those platforms are largely aimed at making friends and advertising, not building your professional network.

Most people don't think of LinkedIn as a place to look at listings or find a real estate agent. They generally visit LinkedIn to network with and learn about other professionals.

For this reason, LinkedIn real estate marketing is a perfect way to engage leads when they're most interested in networking and, hopefully, most interested in learning about your services. If you have a great LinkedIn profile and content, prospects will see you as more professional.

Truth is, LinkedIn is an untapped gold mine.

Their mobile user count is climbing every month, which only makes it easier to reach the people you're trying to reach. Mobile makes it easier for a user to just open the app and scroll through, giving you more opportunities to reach them.

LinkedIn currently reports 645 million total users and 300 million monthly active users who visit daily yet only 3 million users share content on a weekly basis—just 1% of its monthly users.

In October 2018, LinkedIn changed its feed algorithm to help private users get their posts seen while slightly reducing the reach of super-popular "power users."

That's because while total interactions on LinkedIn have increased 50% YoY, most of those interactions were with the top 1% of influencers. This latest update means that all but the largest users and brands on LinkedIn have seen their average reach and engagement improve.

What does this mean for you?

It means if you want to reach more people on LinkedIn, the algorithm changes favor individual content creators (you and me) vs. high profile "influencers." Users who consistently post relevant articles and videos are seeing dramatic increases in reach and engagement on LinkedIn.

Live Video is On LinkedIn!

The company said livestreams have been the most requested feature for the site. Viewers will be able to "like" videos during the stream, while interactive elements will include the ability to submit questions or offer ideas via a comments section, similar to other social media platforms that offer livestreams.

The feature is launching in the U.S. in beta as an invitation-only offering, giving LinkedIn a chance to iron out any wrinkles before rolling it out to the entire community.

According to TechCrunch, LinkedIn is keen to include slickly produced livestreams as opposed to shoddily made productions that have no hope of keeping you engaged. With that goal in mind, it has partnered with a number of livestream services that will help creators produce something worth watching, or, at the very least, with decent production values.

Performing well with the LinkedIn all comes down to relevance of content for your target audience and—like all social platforms—consistency of posting and engaging.

TWITTER

TWITTER IS A social networking and microblogging social media site for news, entertainment, sports, politics, and more. What makes Twitter different from most other social media sites is that it has a strong emphasis on real-time information—things that are happening right now.

Another unique characteristic of Twitter is that it only allows 280 characters in a tweet, unlike most social media sites that have a much higher limit. Twitter messages are limited to 280 characters, and users are also able to upload photos or short videos. Tweets are posted to a publicly available profile or can be sent as direct messages to other users.

IS TWITTER DYING?

IN APRIL 2019, Forbes reported that in the last seven years, Twitter has experienced a slow steady decline in the popularity of its service.[9]

In early 2018, Twitter axed more than 70 million suspicious accounts over several months. This was known as the Twitter Purge. "The health of the public conversation on Twitter remains our greatest priority so people feel safe being a part of the conversation and are able to find credible information on our service," the company writes.

Twitter's third quarter 2019 report states the number of monthly active U.S. Twitter users amounted to 30 million, an increase from 29 million, as compared to 26 million in the same period of the previous year and compared to 29 million in the previous quarter.

Nearly all of Twitter's growth is international. Twitter now has 145 million daily users, up from 115 million one year ago. Similar to monthly users, growth is slow in the US, with about 10 million users in that jump coming from other countries. That number is up 17% since Q3 2018, according to Twitter's Q3 2019 report.

The way you win on Twitter will look very different from the way you win on Facebook or Instagram. To be clear, when we're talk-

---

9. http://bit.ly/2S17kho

ing about generating leads on Twitter, we're talking about *organic* leads

Do agents sell homes through Twitter? Can you originate loans on Twitter? From my research, answer is yes—but the ROI on other social platforms is exponentially greater.

PINTEREST

PINTEREST HAS BECOME a major player both in social networking and in the search world, proving just how important visual content has become on the web. Over 300 million people around the world visit Pinterest each month with over 85 million from the U.S. alone. Pinterest says that 80% of the platform's new sign-ups now come from outside the US.

Pinterest remains substantially more popular with 70% of its user being women.

For adults aged 18–34, or the millennial generation, half of them use Pinterest at least once a month because it inspires them to "make dreams a reality." Perhaps one of those dreams is being inspired to become a first time homeowner?

Pinterest's beautiful and intuitive pin-board platform is one of the most enticing and useful resources for collecting the best images that can be categorized into separate boards.

Similar to Google, Pinterest is actually a search engine. . However, it has better images which is a Real Estate Agent's heaven. Furthermore, the life of a pin, unlike some of the faster-moving platforms, has a really long lifespan. So if you take the time to pin something today, people could still be pinning it even years from now, which would mean a steady flow of traffic for years to come.

With a focus on food, fashion, home decor and parenting, Pinterest is not as shouty as Twitter, as instant as Instagram or as sexy as Snapchat but rather resembles a glossy magazine.

Pinterest CEO Ben Silberman has repeatedly noted that Pinterest is not a social network. The app's various updates and new tools have virtually all related to increased exposure for products and brands, with an eye towards making it the key destination for discovery and purchase.

Pinterest also serves as an awesome place to brand your business. Since the platform is visual, you can easily showcase all of your happy buyers, sellers, and teammates. These photos will humanize your brand and build trust which is essential for the sales process.

It may not give you the reach of Facebook or Instagram, but Pinterest may offer something more valuable –exposure to users who are looking to make buying decisions.

SNAPCHAT

SNAPCHAT IS A social networking app that thrives on instant messaging and is totally mobile-based. It became one of the fastest growing apps out there, building its popularity on the idea of self-destructing "snaps." You can send a photo or short video as a message (a snap) to a friend which automatically disappears a few seconds after they've viewed it.

Unlike Facebook and Twitter, Snapchat is more of a minimalist social network. You can create Snaps, 10-second clips in photo or video format, and Stories, also known as collections of Snaps in chronological order.

Of course, Facebook and Instagram have recently added Stories as well which may prove to be a difficult hurdle for Snapchat to overcome. Within eight months, Instagram Stories surpassed Snapchat's daily active user count.

Snapchat's seeming disregard for its short-term business prospects has been catching up with it, as revealed in its earnings report that the company continues to struggle to bring in advertisers and add users. Snap shares plunged to an all-time low.

The Snapchat fad could finally be over as millions of users keep ditching the app. Daily users have been falling consistently throughout 2019, and one recent report suggested as many as 40% of staffers planned to leave the ailing firm. Snapchat founder, Evan Spiegel, even admitted last year that the app "may never be profitable."

TIKTOK

IF YOU'VE HEARD of TikTok, chances are you've got a teenager somewhere in your life. The app, launched by Chinese company ByteDance (known in China as Douyin) in late 2016, has gone international within the past couple of years.

It was the most installed app in Q1 of 2019 and now boasts over 800 million active monthly users who are spending an incredible amount of tim, approximately 46 minutes per day, consuming videos that are typically only 15 seconds long.

It has been described as a mashup of Vine, Twitter, and Instagram, allowing its 500 million monthly users to create short-form, music-focused videos and edit them with lenses, filters, and Augmented Reality features.

Originally known as Musical.ly, TikTok stepped neatly into the void left by Vine, after its untimely departure in 2017, and has been steadily gaining the attention of young users ever since with its short, highly engaging content. Over 40% of the app's users are between the ages of 10 and 19, making it a prime target for any brands seeking the elusive attention of Gen Z.

Many people believe TikTok is "the next big thing" in the world of social but for the most part, is still uncharted territory when it comes to marketing. It should be looked at with caution, before putting much of your time or emphasis on the platform. TikTok is still quite small, compared to the giants of social media and users can be notoriously fickle; what is hot one day might not be the next.

Will the hype last? According to stats from Trust Insights and Talkwalker, the number of people quitting TikTok is just as noteworthy as the number of people signing up. As reported in The Verge, TikTok recently experienced its first ever growth slowdown on a quarterly basis.

With over 60% of its user base residing in China, TikTok still needs to gain some serious global steam. The real question to ask is: where is your target market, and which content type most aligns with your brand and personality?

MESSENGER APPS AND CHATBOTS

MESSAGING APPS HAVE already passed social media apps in usage, and it seems to be a trend that will dominate 2020. People are moving beyond public posts on social media to private messaging, whether it's simply about reaching their friends or even to stay in touch with their favorite brands.

People and businesses now exchange over 20 billion messages each month on Facebook Messenger, ten times more than they did in 2016

Facebook Messenger and WhatsApp (owned by Facebook) hold the large percentage of the messaging market. WhatsApp is rather unpopular within the United States. In fact, a lot of Americans had never heard of the company before Facebook bought it in 2014.

However, WhatsApp, a global market leader, is slowly seeing rising usage statistics in the US. Many Americans actively use WhatsApp to communicate with friends and family abroad.

The top four messaging apps (Facebook Messenger, WhatsApp, WeChat and Viber) have more monthly active users than three of the top social networking apps (Facebook, Twitter, and Instagram).

They already introduced additional features to go beyond messaging, from Stories and news updates to automated bots for customer service and e-commerce functions.

> "The truth is, the amount of time people spend on messaging apps has grown exponentially and is much higher compared to any other platform, including social media. Brands need to recognize this and adjust accordingly."
>
> Debbi Dougherty
> Head of Marketing
> Viber

Alongside the good old text message, many Americans use Facebook Messenger in order to send messages.

Messaging bots can help reduce the workload, but too much automation can have negative consequences. In a survey conducted by Invoca and Harris Poll, 52% of consumers say they get frustrated when brands don't offer any human interaction.[10] According to GlobalWebIndex's 2020 Consumer Trends report, consumers in the top income bracket are nearly twice as likely to prefer human interaction for customer service.[11]

---

10. http://bit.ly/2uol2Sb
11. http://bit.ly/31yo9mx

WHAT IS A CHATBOT?

A chatbot is a computer program or artificial intelligence which conducts a conversation via auditory or textual methods. Such programs are often designed to convincingly simulate how a human would behave as a conversational partner.

Wikipedia

Bots are programmed to understand questions, provide answers, and execute tasks. From a customer's perspective, they're a friendly and accessible time-saver. Rather than opening an app (let alone downloading one), making a phone call (ugh!), running a search, or loading a webpage, your customer can just type a message like they would to a friend.

Although the technology is still in its early stages of development, messenger bots on websites and in mobile apps will eventually become the standard for consumers. Current usage of Facebook Messenger suggests the future is shifting toward an increasing use of messenger bots by businesses and people:

According to BI Intelligence survey data, Chatbots adoption has already taken off in the US with more than half of its users being between the ages of 18 and 55.[12]

CHATBOTS FOR REAL ESTATE AND MORTGAGE

SIXTY-SEVEN PERCENT OF consumers expect to chat with a business.[13] Homebuyers and sellers, like everyone else, want to connect with you instantly when they have a need. They expect

---

12. http://bit.ly/2SdBWfl
13. http://bit.ly/2UE2UP1

prompt responses from their real estate agent and mortgage professional as well and are comfortable using instant messaging tools in their daily lives.

Emails have been around for decades, and messaging apps are relatively new; however, over 45 PERCENT OF CONSUMERS SAY THEY WOULD CHOOSE THEM OVER EMAIL to get in touch with a business. According to eMarketer, by 2022, more than half of U.S. residents will use a messenger app.[14]

Using chatbots, you can engage with leads, deliver relevant content, have a conversation, and turn visitors into prospects.

SOCIAL MEDIA IS HERE TO STAY

WITH ANY NEW trend or fad, there will surely be a wave of backlash from the general public (and particularly those entrenched in old ways) before acceptance begins to take hold, but, whether you like it or not, social media is here to stay.

Why?

Because it is no longer a trend or fad. It is now a part of our daily lives and culture. Social media is the single-most underpriced, effective, and direct-to-audience form of communication that we have.

Do you have a robust presence on social media? 93% of consumers expect you to have a social media presence. (Cone, Inc.)[15] If not, you are fading away from consumer attention.

---

14. http://bit.ly/390kRVT
15. http://bit.ly/39yFMpt

CHAPTER 5:
THE RISE OF REAL ESTATE DISRUPTORS

A s DISCUSSED IN previous chapters, new technologies have arisen in the last ten years, introducing many 'disruptive' innovations which brought significant change to several industries, even making some obsolete.

Just as Uber and Lyft changed the taxi industry, and web-based companies such as Airbnb are disrupting the hotel industry, the real estate industry is another industry that's vulnerable to information-driven disruption.

The promise of speed, convenience, efficiency, and empowering the consumer to make more informed decisions has been the focus of the industry's latest innovations and where the bulk of investment dollars are going.

Softbank launched the Vision Fund, a nearly $100 billion venture capital fund, with a mission to invest in technology entrepreneurs solving the world's most focal challenges. Real estate companies are now technology companies, and technology companies want more of your information to control your opinion and behavior.

Compass, the New York City-headquartered real estate brokerage that has been on a cross-country acquisition spree, and Opendoor, the San Francisco-based online homebuyer and seller targeting 50+ markets, each announced funding rounds worth $400 million a piece from Softbank.

That funding round comes on top of the previous $450 million that the Vision Fund plowed into Compass, as well as a number of other eye-popping bets on real estate tech.

Due to the fact that the residential real estate industry in the U.S. is so large, with many different specialized sub-markets (construction, financing, selling, etc.), SoftBank sees opportunities to build successful, profitable and disruptive new businesses that leverage technology across the entire real estate supply chain.

It has invested $865 million in the construction-tech startup Katerra, as well a $120 million round in Lemonade, a tech-powered provider of homeowners and renters' insurance.

Zillow has definitely succeeded in disrupting the real estate industry. According to its Q3 2019 earnings report, Zillow Group brands' mobile apps and websites reached more than 196 million unique monthly users during the third quarter of 2019.

Zillow reports that 50% of site visitors intend to sell or buy. It maintains a database of 110 million U.S. homes and 186 homes per second are viewed across its family of websites apps and portals. According to Zillow, many consumers visit Zillow's websites to view information about homes for sale or rent that are listed with brokers or the homes' owners.

The company's five year revenue target is $22 billion, of which $2 billion will be from agent, lender, rental, new construction and other leads and services, and $20 billion is forecasted to be from buying and selling homes via its Zillow Offers service.

Inman reported in 2019 that co-founder Gary Keller proclaimed Keller Williams as a tech company. "We are a technology company. No. 1 that means we build the technology. No. 2 that means we hire the technologists ... We are not a real estate company anymore."

The rise of "Hybrid Brokerages" provide an alternative to the traditional broker commission and service model, offering every-thing from discounted listing fees and buyer rebates to innovative technology and salaried agents.

"The old idea that real estate is never going to change, that we're going to pay 6 percent, is completely untrue," argues Glenn Kel-man, the CEO of Seattle-based Redfin, a publicly traded broker-age whose calling card is lower commissions.

Redfin hasn't been shy in proclaiming its disruptive role. When it registered to go public, the company's filing declared: "And this is our mission in a sales-mad, baloney-gorged world, to be the truth-teller, the fee-squeezer, the game-changer."

Redfin's goal, says CEO Glenn Kelman, is to use technology to make the process of buying and selling a home better, faster, and less expensive.

Is Redfin a hot technology company with the potential to disrupt how Americans buy and sell homes or is it just another discount residential brokerage?

To homebuyers who use a Redfin agent, its RedfinRefund pro-gram touts an average refund of $1,700 back to the buyer from agent commissions. When you sell with Redfin, you pay a 1.5% listing fee. When you use Redfin to buy and sell a home within one year, you pay a 1% listing fee. If you sell first, you'll initially pay a 1.5% listing fee. Then, when you buy with a Redfin Agent, RedFin will pay back the half percent. *Restrictions apply.

With RedFin, sellers get all the digital bells and whistles for that price, including free professional photos, a 3D walk-through, and a digital marketing campaign.

If you show an interest in buying, Redfin will send you links to houses in markets you've expressed an interest in. If it determines that a property you're interested in is likely to sell soon, it will send you an alert. If you want to move quickly, Redfin lets you schedule a tour with the click of a button.

Redfin's technology platform has expanded to include virtually every element of the home-buying process—from search to closing.

The company has established its own mortgage company and makes direct loans. It can act as an escrow agent through its title and settlement service business and even buys homes directly from homeowners interested in a quick sale under its new RedfinNow program. Redfin launched its mortgage operations in 2017 and claims to be the "fastest, easiest way for homebuyers to receive a quote, get pre-approved and finance their home purchase," the company said.

THE RISE OF THE IBUYERS

AN IBUYER IS a company that will make you an offer on your home within minutes (or days), sight unseen, based on a proprietary valuation model. When selling to an IBUYER, the other side of the transaction is a company or an investor.

There's no need to stage the home, have neighbors traipsing through an open house, or worry about the buyer's loan falling through.

The main players in the U.S. include Opendoor, Zillow, RedfinNow Offerpad, and Knock —allowing home sellers to close in days instead of months by directly buying homes at a (mostly) fair price and flipping them back on the market.

Realogy Holdings announced that one of its franchises, Coldwell Banker, will be launching a direct buying business in several markets. Coldwell is debuting a "quick-cash sales program" called cataLIST Cash Offer where homeowners can get offers for their homes within 24 hours. Coldwell Banker says real estate professionals will remain a central figure in this new sales process.

Keller Williams is the latest brokerage to jump into the iBuyer game is expanding markets through its partnership with OFFER-PAD.

Its program is still in its testing stage but has closed over 100 transactions. Through initial market testing, they have confirmed that consumers want an agent to help them through all their options available.

The CEO of Knock, another competitor to Zillow Offers, predicted that in 10 years, more than 50 percent of home sales will go toward iBuyers.

THE TOP THREE PLAYERS CURRENTLY IN THE IBUYER SPACE.

OPENDOOR IS the pioneer and current market leader, reportedly purchasing more than $2.5 billion in homes annually with a $2 billion valuation. It also recently began offering mortgage and title services to buyers.

Opendoor pays agent commissions and will also pay referral fees to real estate agents.

Opendoor buys homes using debt from institutional investors, makes light repairs, and then puts the homes it has purchased back on the market, typically within a week or so. All offers from Opendoor investors are good for five days.

Opendoor has been described as a flipper, but it's not trying to make money by rehabbing homes. With Opendoor, you'll pay a service charge vs a listing fee. According to their website, on average, the service charge is 6-7%, but it could be lower or higher.

The service charge varies based on how long they expect it will take to sell your home and the minor repairs needed.

After viewing the home online, buyers can get in to see it, with or without their own agents, between 6 a.m. and 9 p.m. seven days a week. They open the house with a smartphone app.

If the buyer has an agent, Opendoor will give that agent the usual commission, typically 3 percent. If the buyer has no agent, Opendoor keeps the full commission.

Agents who are already working with sellers can also get an offer from Opendoor, and if the seller accepts it, the agent will get a referral fee which Opendoor would not disclose.

Opendoor's "trade-in" program lets homeowners sell their home and buy a new one from Opendoor all at once.

For families that are growing or changing, where more bedrooms are a necessity or additional living space is desirable, Opendoor has partnered with Lennar Homes offering a unique New Home Trade-Up Program. In one seamless transaction, you can arrange for the purchase of your current home from Opendoor and upgrade your family to a brand new Lennar "move-up" home, using your earned equity as a down payment on the upgrade.

It also offers a money-back guarantee that promises a full refund to buyers should they sour on the home they bought from Opendoor.

All-day open houses, end-to-end software, mortgage brokerage, and looped-in vendors, including mortgage services, are just a few of the perks that Opendoor provides to homebuyers.

Where Opendoor falls short are proprietary channels of online acquisition. Without a best-in-class search experience, such as Redfin or Zillow, Opendoor will need to double down on paid acquisition channels for finding sellers and source a greater proportion of buyers through the MLS—which means paying a full buyer agent commission.

Zillow changed up its business in model in 2018 and is rapidly expanding its Zillow Offers service, directly buying and selling homes, across the U.S.

Zillow offers sellers two options: to buy the house outright with a cash offer, also known as a "Zillow Offer," or to connect sellers with a "Premier" agent if they want their home listed on the open market.

The company confirms that it is running tests on Zillow.com and its mobile apps that will show its own for-sale homes at the top of its home search pages, ahead of other competing for-sale listings.

On homes that aren't owned by Zillow, browsers are greeted by the message, "Buying but need to sell first? Get a Zillow Offer for your home," under the listing photos.

In fact, Zillow believes that its iBuyer program ends up being an "excellent" source of leads for real estate agents. Only seven months after the launch of Zillow's iBuyer, Zillow had already received offer requests from 20,000 homeowners yet since launching, they're purchase rate consistently hovers around 6%.

This means most sellers currently decline Zillow's offer, and, when this happens, Zillow refers them to their real estate agent partners. Zillow Offers also serves as a massive seller intent machine, then routes those potential listings to its agents who list and close from there.

Mikel DelPrete is a global real estate thought leader, tech strategist, and a scholar-in-residence at the University of Colorado Boulder. His research delivers insights and analysis into the world of iBuyers.

Dubbed, the 'iBuyer whisperer,' his iBuyer Report analyzes the data behind Zillow Offers, Opendoor, Offerpad and the growing trend of all-cash offers online.

In his research, Mike points out that the iBuyer business model could be considered as Zillow's "Zestimate 2.0" – the natural starting point for determining your home's value. What's more accurate than *an actual offer on your home*?

The iBuyer business model generates an incredible amount of seller leads: consumers that are interesting in seller their house.

If you're thinking about Zillow and Opendoor as iBuyers and you're not thinking about seller leads, you're thinking about it the wrong way. Seller leads are the real billion-dollar opportunity.

Zillow will also be partnering with local real estate brokerages to serve as the designated real estate outlets for its direct buying program.

Startup Zavvie.com has added a new layer of transparency to the Instant Offer process with its Offer Optimizer, delivering side-by-side comparisons, built-in logic, and straight-forward explanations of the home selling experience.

Consumers can see a side-by-side comparison online of how much money they make after closing with different national iBuyers—including Zillow, as well as Opendoor, Offerpad, and Redfin Now. Then, Zavvie does one better. It lists local iBuyer firms and has even begun partnering with local brokerages, helping them with an iBuyer Toolkit to offer a local iBuyer alternative to compete with these national firms.

ZILLOW MORTGAGE HAS ARRIVED

WHEN ZILLOW announced their acquisition of Mortgage Lenders of America (MLOA), the purchase is said to boost

Zillow's "Offers" program, offering mortgages for home buyers making offers on the site.

Zillow announced that it is launching its own mortgage lending operation, which it is calling ZILLOW HOME LOANS.

> "Getting a mortgage is often the hardest, most complicated part of buying a home," said Greg Schwartz, Zillow Group president of media and marketplaces. "We acquired MLOA, which we will rebrand in 2019, so we could streamline, shorten and simplify the home-buying process for consumers who purchase homes through Zillow Offers."

For years, prospective homebuyers could search for a mortgage through Zillow's site, as lenders paid to have their interest rates and terms listed on Zillow's mortgage marketplace.

Now, they'll have a new competitor: Zillow itself.

Zillow explained that owning a mortgage lender will allow it to develop new tools and partnership opportunities, including for real estate brokers with existing in-house mortgage operations or mortgage affiliates and its existing mortgage advertisers.

The company added that the use of Zillow Home Loans is "not restricted" to Zillow Offers home sales. According to Zillow, borrowers may still use Zillow's mortgage marketplace to shop for a lender and loan for any home purchase or refinanced loan. Consumers have the option of choosing to work with the best offer and then can rate the experience afterwards.

THE INTERNET IS THE TOP OF THE SALES FUNNEL

IN SHORT, ALMOST everyone starts shopping online, and a vast majority are going to Zillow. So, in many respects, Zillow is at the top of the sales funnel for home lending transactions.

Zillow has the distribution (consumers); it has Premier Agents in every market, and it is working with national investors who could theoretically go anywhere.

According to the J.D. Power Primary Mortgage Origination Study,[1] more than 50% of buyers said they received a mortgage lender recommendation from their agent. Out of that group, roughly 37% of first-time buyers and 28% for repeat buyers used that recommendation with first-time buyers in particular, indicating that referrals from a real estate agent are one of the top influences in their lender choice.

However, these same consumers also indicate that they are using Zillow (59% of all purchase customers and 67% of first-time buyers). With Zillow engaging in an initial lending discussion at the onset of the home-buying process, it is conceivable to think that they could set themselves up as their own referral engine.

Let's assume that 50% of that group is visiting Zillow—that means they are starting with 40% of all the purchase borrowers engaging with them online, in some form or fashion. If we then assume that they are successful at capturing mindshare of 5% of this group to win their mortgage business, that would mean they'd have 2% of all purchase loans and would likely make them a top 20 lender in the United States.

However, consumers still crave personal interaction throughout the mortgage origination process, which is especially true, as consumers prefer a personal follow-up after an initial inquiry.

In fact, J.D. Power released its 2019 U.S. Primary Mortgage Origination Satisfaction Survey data, revealing that although the usage

---

1. http://bit.ly/2ULph5f

of digital channels increased, only 3% of consumers rely exclusively on digital self-service channels. Furthermore, satisfaction peaked when consumers spoke with lenders either in-person or on the phone as they applied for a mortgage.

There are lots of unknowns here, and it still unclear what this all could mean down the line. That said, it is hard to ignore the potential effect that "Zillow Mortgage" could have on further disrupting the real estate and mortgage industry in the future.

The need for real estate and mortgage professionals that don't provide anything of true value is diminishing rapidly. This isn't to say you aren't needed. You certainly are.

It's likely that even as iBuying grows in popularity, the partnerships with real estate agents will continue to be a part of their business model for the foreseeable future.

Based on transaction volume in 2019, the largest iBuyer companies are Opendoor, Zillow and Offerpad.

There is a second-tier of iBuyer companies, including Redfin, Perch, Knock, and others — but none have the national footprint, funding firepower, and transaction volumes of the leaders. Opendoor and Zillow account for roughly 86 percent of iBuyer transaction volumes.

So we've looked at the trends driving the digital real estate disruption. The question is: what are YOU doing to evolve and innovate?

In Part II, we'll look at how you can "disrupt proof" your business by embracing technology and positioning yourself early in the consumer's journey to become known, get chosen and thrive during the digital real estate shift. Are you ready? Let's read on!

PART II:
BECOMING A MODERN REAL ESTATE AND MORTGAGE PROFESSIONAL

C ONSUMERS TODAY HAVE counteless options of Mortgage Lenders and Real Estate Agents to choose from and nearly unlimited ways to shop rates and find homes without needing you.

To be relevant today and get chosen, we must first become known and win the customer early.

Part II will guide you through developing your personal brand, effective content marketing, lead generation, and modern marketing strategies to get known, get clients and future-proof your business.

CHAPTER 6:
THE BRAND CALLED YOU

THERE ARE A lot of real estate agents and mortgage lenders out there. It's a noisy world that's getting noisier with iBuyers and discounters creating a more fragmented market as we learned in Chapter 5.

Buyers today are savvy. They can tell whether the company, and the people in it are congruent.

They seek out, resonate with, and tend to be loyal to companies and people that place human connection above closing a transaction.

> "In the absence of branding, all you're left with is marketing the same things your competitors have. When you do that, you will always be perceived as just like them. When you successfully create a brand, you will stand out. You will lead. You will develop fans. You will create clarity for your customers and help them understand and feel great about their place in the world."
>
> Marc Davison, Chief Creative, 1000 Watt

When I teach Personal Branding Mastery classes for agents and lenders, I ask the audience: "How many of you have a personal brand?"

Most of the room looks unsure and confused. They're thinking logos, slogans, property types or "first time homebuyer specialist." For real estate agents and mortgage lenders, branding is a much more personal thing than a logo or what color to make your business cards. Here's what I tell attendees of my Personal Branding Mastery classes:

You already have a personal brand. If you're not branding yourself, someone else is doing it for you.

It's what you do [or don't do] every day. It's how you show up online, your timely follow-up and response times, your customer experience, and the feelings people have and how they describe what its like working with you.

While the term personal brand is tainted and abused, what it stands for is not.

What is a personal brand, exactly?

Personal branding means having the reputation, authority, and presence to connect with people, build trust and relationships that lead to business.

Best-selling author Mark Schaefer, points out in his latest book, *Marketing Rebellion,* that in today's world, "the most human company wins."

This human connection is what we crave—what we have ALWAYS desired—even in an overwhelming content world of online videos, social selfies and Instagram filters.

WHAT ARE YOU KNOWN FOR?

HERE IS A business truth: People buy from who they know, like, and trust. You're in a business that requires you to be known, be like-able and be trustworthy.

It's not enough to just be known for being an agent or loan officer. That's not unique and doesn't create authority or human connection in and of itself.

In his book *So Good They Can't Ignore You*, Georgetown University professor, Cal Newport, wrote the formula for branding success isn't simply finding a passion or even a niche; it's finding the magical intersection of *place* and *space* that will give you the best shot at becoming known and successful.

Let's take a closer look.

Place is a SUSTAINABLE INTEREST and what you want to be *known* for.

Space is an uncontested or UNDER-OCCUPIED niche with enough people to matter.

A sustainable interest is something that you love, that you'll enjoy for years. It's also a subject matter you want to be known for. Your sustainable interest is *not* necessarily your passion.

Let me explain.

I'm passionate about music and playing the guitar. I could decide to pursue my *passion* for music, take guitar lessons, practice hours per day, and join a band. We'll call ourselves Old Guys Rock!

That sounds fun, except I'm not that good of a musician, and dogs howl when I sing. There may be a small audience on the weekend local bar circuit, but that's not going to help me achieve my life goals.

Music and guitar are passions and hobbies, but do I really want to become *known* for being the middle-aged, mediocre, slightly grey-haired rocker who can barely play guitar and can't sing to save his own life?

The most important question is: Are these passions sustainable interests that will take me to the next level of my career? Is there a big enough audience to matter?

In the case of pursuing my passion for music, no. It's just a hobby.

Pursuing that passion would mean abandoning all the other things I'm good at, all the skills I've accumulated for decades.

Let's take a look at other areas of my life that might be more sustainable:

- I have almost 30 years of experience in sales and marketing
- I studied under Tony Robbins during his early career
- I'm a skilled public speaker and facilitator
- I've been a sales trainer and coach at large organizations
- I host a podcast that reaches thousands of people every month
- I have the heart of a teacher
- I have deep experience within the real estate industry

Teaching people the truth about branding, sales, and digital marketing and specifically about creating meaningful connections and growing a business seems like a much more sustainable interest than playing in a local bar band on weekends.

It's something I can truly be known for and enjoy doing every day—over the long haul. Even more important, it provides me with a sense of fulfillment and making a real difference which fuels my purpose in life.

It is my PLACE where I have sustainable interest and what I want to be known for.

I'll assume because you're reading this book, your *place* that gives you sustainable interest is the business of real estate or mortgage.

Congratulations! Helping people buy, sell and finance homes makes a real difference in people's lives. Choosing a specific niche—as you'll soon see—gives your personal brand the power to rise above the sea of sameness in your space and *become known*.

CHOOSING YOUR SPACE

SO YOUR *PLACE* is real estate or mortgage. The next question to answer is where is your SPACE? This is the space where you'll build a community of people who know like and trust you.

Remember how we define space? An uncontested or *under-occupied* niche with enough people to matter. In today's hyper competitive world, it may seem that there aren't many under-occupied niches left. The truth is most people are generalists and do not have a niche focus, leaving opportunity for those who decide to pursue a specific niche.

FIRST MOVER ADVANTAGE

THE MOST OBVIOUS approach for success in a space is to be the first person to establish a foothold in a niche. Often, being first is more influential than being the best!

Being in real estate and mortgage means you already have competition, but most agents and lenders are not taking advantage of under-occupied niches. You may not have first mover advantage, but there is an almost unlimited amount of under-occupied niches, and many may have nothing to actually do with real estate itself.

Let's look at some examples of niches.

1. SOCIAL NICHES

SOCIAL NICHES ARE those that you create in your non-real estate life.

Do you have kids involved in sports? Do you coach Little League? Forming a niche within the Little League or sports community can be a fantastic opportunity to gain clientele from the parents of kids.

This is leveraging your sphere of influence for your business. Sponsor a team or tournament, or bring in a guest trainer, sponsor special events for the kids like movie showings at the local theatre or the field for the team so that you can brand these teams and events with your business, thus connecting your business with the success of your children and your clients' children.

2. GEOGRAPHIC FARM NICHES

GEOGRAPHIC NICHES (ALSO known as a farm)—is focusing on a particular area, neighborhood, development, or part of town—and can be incredibly powerful. Success in this type of niche, more than others, requires two things: focus and expertise.

This isn't to say you shouldn't take business outside of your farm. You may want to consider referring some of that business out, allowing you to focus your efforts. Gaining expertise in a very particular area and then marketing that expertise to the area is more likely to result in new business than marketing yourself as a generalist to a much larger area.

Potential geographic farm niches include: waterfront, beach, vacation, downtown, rural, mountain, and so many more.

3. REAL ESTATE NICHES

REAL ESTATE NICHES can be combined with geographic farm niches and can very lucrative for your business. There are so many potential niches that it is almost impossible not to find one that will interest you. Potential real estate niches include waterfront, equestrian, luxury, new construction, condos, historic homes, vacation, downtown and so many more.

Husband and wife agent team Nick Constantino and Karren Winther live in Fort Langley, BC. They are lifelong horse owners and competitors. As their website says; "we sell country lifestyles" and "being lifelong horse owners makes us very aware of the needs of acreage buyers and sellers."

If I am a homeowner with an equestrian property, then I am going to want someone who knows all of the issues surrounding this type of property, not only because they are more likely to be connected to someone interested in purchasing an equestrian property, but also because their intimate knowledge creates trust in handling the transaction.

Here are some examples of Real Estate + geographic farm niches:

- Downtown condos, in a specific price range, in a specific building
- Equestrian land buyers, looking for five or more acres
- Senior homebuyers requiring single level homes, close to amenities
- Historic homes with restoration potential

- Luxury properties in highly desired, gated communities

4. LOAN PRODUCT NICHES

WHILE MOST LENDERS have access to the same loans, you can become known for having expertise in certain products.

Jeff Onofrio is Managing Director, Renovation, Construction and National Production for Mortgage Possible headquartered in New Jersey.

He launched RenovateThis.com, as a home improvement video blog and podcast that helps homeowners and investors create wealth with real estate and rehab loan programs.

Jeff took his previous company from being non-existent in renovation loans to being ranked at the highest point #6 in the nation, based upon the FHA 203k endorsement schedule.

Do you have an affinity to serve the Veteran community?

Having grown up in a military household, Rick Elmendorf with Caliber Home Loans always had an admiration for the men and women who serve in the armed forces, which has inspired him to help thousands of military personnel obtain VA financing. Rick ranks as the #1 VA lender for purchase volume in Metro DC, funding over $80 million in VA loans in 2019.

5. DEMOGRAPHIC NICHES

ANOTHER WAY TO stand out from the crowd is to market to a subset of the population. If done correctly, this targeted group of people will immediately self-identify and resonate with your brand.

Here's a few examples to get you started:

- First Time Home Buyers
- Multigenerational Families
- Hispanics (the nations largest minority group)
- Newlyweds
- Divorcing Couples
- Singles
- Veterans
- Investors
- Single Parents
- Empty Nesters
- First Responders

REAL WORLD EXAMPLES

At Divorce Mortgage Advisors in Burlingame, CA, their mission is simple. "We strive to be a catalyst for meaningful and informative conversations about how to successfully settle real estate matters in divorce."

Co-founder Ross Garcia obtained his Certified Divorce Lending (CDLP) designation, and Jason Crowley is a Certified Divorce Financial Analyst (CDFA). Their consumer driven website survivedivorce.com helps them get discovered in Google search, builds their audience, and drives leads.

Chris Spivey is a former EMT and a real estate agent in North Carolina. His niche is First Responders. He created the "Wilmington Area's First Responders Only Real Estate Program." The purpose is "to help, give back and protect those who protect us." They don't just help first responders buy and sell real estate....their mission is to donate thousands of dollars to local and first-responder related charities each year.

His website and social media presence include photos of him involved in local events supporting police, fire and rescue personnel. Many of the photos show Chris holding oversized checks of money raised through his involvement. His personal brand is not just a real estate agent. He's part of an exclusive community of people who share a strong, personal bond.

4. BECOME A COMMUNITY EXPERT

A GREAT WAY to blend your PLACE (sustainable interest) with SPACE (community of people) is to become the go-to resource for local community events and happenings. This is a great way to not only show your activity in the local market, but most homebuyers and sellers want a real estate professional who lives, works and plays within the areas they service!

Jason Farris is a forward thinking agent in Fresno, CA. He created a simple website called FRESYES.com that really highlights all the positive things that Fresno has to offer.

When asked why, Jason says: "I want people to know that Fresno is a great place to live, you don't have to be in Los Angeles or San Francisco."

He features local businesses, community events, and even has residents contributing content to the site as well. He also features properties on the site, and the traffic he's built on the site has been a huge benefit to his sellers. His FRESYES Facebook page has over 25,000 actively engaged followers.

Jonathan McKinnies with Hallmark Home Mortgage decided to become the "digital mayor" of his town of Michiana Indiana. He launched Michiana LivingTV as a resource for locals to stay informed about everything in and around Michiana! Their mission is to "provide great quality content that showcases the beauty of Michiana!"

Whether that's a great new brewery opening up, upcoming festivals in town, or the best local place to eat a steak; if it is important to the community, Michiana LivingTV will be there.

Jonathan has invited his local agents to co-host episodes which gives them exposure and creates a strong partnership between Jonathan, his local agents and influential people in his local community.

Michiana LivingTV was launched in December, 2018 and is building a buzz in the community. Each of their videos get thousands of views on Facebook, building their local brand awareness and positioning Jonathan and his mortgage team as influential local residents who also happen to provide mortgage financing.

You can hear Jonathan's interview on the Mortgage Marketing Radio Podcast, Episode #152. www.mortgagemarketinginstitute.com/152

CHOOSING YOUR NICHE

Contrary to what many believe, when you narrow your focus on serving a particular niche, your business will grow. Here's why:

- You'll become an authority.

- Your brand will have more value.

- Your marketing will focus on your area of expertise.

- Your lead generation will produce more highly qualified leads.

- You'll enjoy your job more.

To discover your niche, find something you have sustainable interest about and are actively involved in (or something you want to learn more about or get involved in) then become a known authority in that.

HOW TO BECOME KNOWN

LET ME START off by saying, when I say "known," I don't mean "famous." This is not about turning you into the next overnight YouTube sensation or getting your Instagram followers to one million.

This is about truly becoming known in your field. Social Media can certainly be a part of that process, but there is so much more to it.

By being a known authority and establishing thought leadership in your chosen niche, people will be more likely to trust and choose you.

I often ask attendees of my classes and workshops: "what's more important—being well known or being knowledgeable?"

The spirited debates begin to fill the room. The real answer is both. The challenge is, as we mentioned, you're in a business that requires you to first *become known* before you can apply your knowledge.

How do you rise above the noise, become known, and get people to choose you? What will you be known for? What can you do that's uniquely you? Why would someone read your post or watch your video rather than the many existing voices competing for their attention?

Let's take a look at SIX DIFFERENT strategies for how to become *known* in your space, among your community of people. Stay with me here, and you'll hear the stories of agents and loan officers who, through persistence, learning and self-discovery, became known and created a thriving business they enjoy and find meaningful purpose in.

Six Ways to Become Known

1. DEVELOP A UNIQUE STYLE OR POINT OF VIEW

LIKE THE DISTINCTIVE sound of a singers voice, it's possible for you to stand out in a noisy world by having your own recognizable style or viewpoint. People have access to the same information today. What get's them to follow and listen to *you* is YOUR perspective or how you deliver that information in a unique or engaging way.

Sean Cahan, President and producing Loan Originator of Cornerstone Mortgage Group in San Diego, branded himself as "The Mortgage Geek." Rather than conform to the traditionally corporate world of mortgages, Cahan found a way to use his personal talents and personality to build a unique, recognizable brand.

Dressed in full character with taped glasses, greased back hair, and zany skits, The Mortgage Geek educates and entertains his community about mortgage and housing related topics, keeping them engaged and eager to see what he'll do next.

Topics The Mortgage Geek explores on his weekly videos range from: "Do You Suffer from E.D. (Escrow Delay)? to Fannie Mae lending guideline changes with Sean dressed as "Fannie Mae" in full wig, dress and lipstick, texting and calling The Mortgage Geek to "take her back" with her recent, more "friendly" lending updates.

Does "The Mortgage Geek's" sometimes irreverent style appeal to everyone? No. He's received his fair share of critics, but Sean recognizes that his unique style will both attract and repel—and that's ok.

YOUR PERSONAL BRAND CAN'T BE FOR EVERYONE. Your personal brand should be an extension of who you are. Sean says "The Mortgage Geek is an extension of my personality, just with some glasses on it."

Sean's leadership has also helped Cornerstone Mortgage Group morph from being a single local bank to a nationwide lender with fifteen branches, licensed in 33 states. He manages Cornerstone's operations at the top, but he's also still on the ground, personally closing more than $134 million in volume and has been the top producer at the company for the past three years—having fun along the way!

Finding the right "voice" for your content may take time at the beginning of your journey. Your tone is discovered through practice, feedback, and the occasional divine inspiration. It might be tempting to try to sound like someone else, but that will come across as disingenuous and is likely to get tiresome.

Finding a unique style or point of view is about having the courage to let your true self shine. You probably already have an idea of the "voice" of other leaders in your space. How can you insert your personality to stand out in your own, unique way?

Joanne Littman began her real estate career just five years ago in the competitive market of Westlake Village, CA. A friend asked if she was going to keep her pink hair highlights now that she was an agent.

Her reply? "I will make no apologies for who I am."

She authentically shares her daily struggles and triumphs and has developed her personal brand known as "That Girl" Real Estate. Her Instagram profile @joanne_littman takes followers behind the scenes as she door knocks weekly, and with each closed transaction, buys a new pair of "escrow shoes." When I last spoke with her, Joanne's personable engagement on social media generated 21 referrals and six closings in addition to her other business.

2. GO 'ALL-IN' ON ONE SOCIAL PLATFORM WITHIN YOUR NICHE

KARIN CARR RELOCATED her real estate business from California to Savannah, Georgia to be closer to family. "When you get somewhere new, you're basically a brand-new agent all over again," Carr states.

She started in her new market deciding to go 'all -in' using YouTube, because, in her opinion, YouTube is a very under-utilized platform. It's the second-largest search engine in the world, owned by the first-largest Google, so many agents who are doing video aren't using YouTube.

Her YouTube channel, Georgia Coast Homes, has over 5,600 subscribers, features over 187 videos and has racked up over 257,000 total video views to date.

Karin believes as we head into the shifting market, agents need to be able to generate their own business. "If you're buying leads, they'll get more and more expensive as the market shifts. I feel like you can't be dependent on somebody else to be giving you business; you have to go out there and find it on your own."

For the last year and a half, Karin has been uploading one video a week. Now, she's pushing it up to two videos a week; the more content you can put out there, the faster your channel will grow, and the more people will see it. If somebody Googles something like "relocating to Savannah," Karin's videos dominate the search results both on Google and YouTube.

Karin says that because prospects are watching her videos, when they connect with her over the phone, they often say: "we've been watching your videos, we feel like we already know you and we're ready to buy."

Karin's consistency has paid off. Every week, she receives an average of five high-intent, organic leads who've watched her videos and are ready to buy a home. In 2019, Karin closed 19 of 31 transactions directly from people finding her YouTube channel with zero advertising and very little selling.

KARIN'S WINNING BUSINESS, BECAUSE PEOPLE ARE CHOOSING HER.

They're not inquiring about a property, and she's not competing against other agents. People who consume her videos build a personal connection with Karin. They get to see her engaging personality, her knowledge of the local area, and people trust that Karin is this right agent for them.

Nicole Rueth, Producing Branch Manager with Fairway Mortgage in Denver, is ranked among the top 100 Mortgage Advisors in the country, and she's leading the way with her YouTube channel. Nicole's "Mortgage Education" playlist has over 100 videos, and her "Realtor Education" playlist has more than 120. In two years, she's uploaded over 250 videos!

How does Nicole respond to competing against market disruptors like Zillow or Quicken Loans?

"They've always existed, they will always exist, and while the pace of business is speeding up, clients don't always want speed. They want answers, they want their hands held, and they want to be educated not only on how to buy homes but how to make prudent financial decisions."

"I can't play Quicken's or Zillow's game. I'm not going to win. But they can't play mine. That's the difference. I'm playing the game at a level that they don't even know because I'm educating my clients at a level that their call center employees can never do."

Nicole maintains a consistent weekly schedule, posting two videos every week to YouTube- one for agents and one for consumers. She uses a variety of video styles—mobile, green screen, at home, at the office, in the car (safely parked!), and more. She dominates her market by helping people better understand how they can generate wealth by educating them through video.

3. DOMINATE A CONTENT TYPE

REAL ESTATE AGENT Jesse Peters—a.k.a Mr. Social Savvy in Winnipeg, Canada—is a prime example of a real estate professional who's created a personal brand through the power of social media, and, for most of that time, he's embraced the power of video.

Although he's only been in the industry for just about six years, Jesse knew that he would eventually grow a large network if he shared valuable content on platforms like Facebook in a way that also expresses his personality. By building an identity people could connect with, he was able to not only achieve a larger following but also start to generate business from his use of social media videos and newfound clientele.

Operating under the Social Savvy® brand, he spends much of his video time showcasing Winnipeg—its unique neighborhoods and community. Jesse kept running into situations where so many people would like a home but, not be sold on a neighborhood.

As a result, he started creating neighborhood videos to highlight the top five features, as well as the current market in that specific area. His endeavor into video is part of the reason Jesse sold three homes in his first week as a real estate agent and hasn't slowed his pace since.

Jesse gets phone calls every week from people who explain how their home has been on the market for a little too long and ask for his help to "clean up the mess." He says an agent can easily receive listing requests when it is obvious that the agent is capable of producing content, creating videos and giving them the best opportunity for their home to be seen and given exposure or as Jesse calls it "seen, showcased and Socially Sold®."

Jess also creates client testimonial videos, open house invite videos, buyer love letter videos, and "socially sold" videos as well. He explains how creating more than just listing videos has allowed him to showcase himself to his potential clients, and help them decide if they "know, like, and trust" him enough to bring him on to help them buy or sell their home.

Jesse explains that "every single home I am given the opportunity to sell, whether it's priced at $20,000 or $1.5 million, get it's very own listing video. It's a video that allows us to showcase the lifestyle of a home, pros of a home, and a view of the home from their standpoint that photos can't show you."

Jesse describes how he mainly utilizes live social videos for open houses, answering questions, or comments in real time like "could you show us the kitchen again," or "what condition is the roof in?" This type of interaction enhances the viewers experience. He promotes the "live showing," using both Facebook ads and organic posts, in case someone has a busy week and can't make it to the actual showing in person.

Within his first few years, Jesse's focus on video led to him being ranked in the top 2% of agents in his province for multiple years; he was recently awarded RE/MAX Hall of Fame status. He plays an active role in his community was recently nominated for the Top 40 people Under 40 in Winnipeg.

4. TRY A NEW OR DIFFERENT CONTENT FORM

EVERYONE IS FIGHTING for customer attention. Maybe you've tried some of the traditional ways of reaching your potential customers like cold-calling, door knocking, or even more modern methods like social media and Facebook ads.

What if you could speak to your potential clients every single day, right in their own home?

Now, it's possible to do just that with your own Alexa Flash Briefing delivered over Amazon's smart speakers, including the Echo and Dot.

Essentially, a Flash Briefing is like a "brief" podcast episode. Share community updates, tips on the home-buying or selling process, market updates, local happenings, highlight local businesses or notify your audience of new listings available; all through their Amazon Echo or Dot device!

If you don't like a particular briefing, you can say, "Skip that one," or "Next." To subscribe to a flash briefing, a user can say: "Alexa, add Mortgage Marketing Radio to my Flash Briefings."

Although a briefing can be as long as 10 minutes, the briefings that people stay subscribed to are almost always about 2-3 minutes. You can do your flash briefings hourly, daily or weekly, but I recommend daily to build your audience engagement and drive reviews of your Flash Briefing on Amazon.

How do you create your own Flash Briefing?

To create a new flash briefing, first you need a free Amazon developer account at developer.amazon.com. You'll see Amazon Alexa as the first choice on the page. There's a pretty straightforward creation and submission process.

Once you've created your account, you then start an Alexa Skill. Alexa skills are essentially apps that enable Amazon's voice assistant to perform certain tasks which include delivering your Flash Briefings via Amazon's smart speakers, Echo or Dot.

According to Amazon, as of January 2019, there are now more than 80,000 skills but only ~ 8,000 flash briefings worldwide available in the Alexa Skills store. For every 80 podcasts out there, there is one flash briefing, which illustrates the opportunity right now for early adopters.

Some skills can tell you the tide times for the beach, others can book reservations at your favorite restaurant, or tell a daily joke, but *your* Alexa Skill will play the latest episodes of *your* Flash Briefing.

> Pro tip: Give away Echo devices as a promotion or post closing gifts, and you've got a a built-in listener to your Flash Briefings!

Once you have your Alexa Skill enabled, come up with a title, a short description and relevant keywords. These will help you get found when people search for Alexa Skills that have the words real estate or mortgage, or include your local community, city or town.

To create an Alexa flash briefing, you record and upload an audio file to a hosting provider like Soundupnow.com who will feed your audio to Amazon.

An Alexa flash briefing is available for only 24 hours and then disappears. However, you can batch-process your audio briefings for several days in one sitting, which streamlines the work of delivering a flash briefing every day.

People often listen to their flash briefings while they're getting up and ready in the morning. After you say, "Alexa, play my flash briefing," the briefings which you've enabled, such as weather or business, begin playing one at a time.

Each briefing typically begins with the name of the content producer so, in the case of my own flash briefing, Alexa will say "from Las Vegas Real Estate, here's today's update.

Flash briefings are still in their infancy and consumer attention hasn't shifted away from established social media platforms in a significant way yet. Therefore, your focus should be on building up your awareness where consumer attention is happening. If Amazon decides to flex its muscle, Flash Briefings could be become another channel for becoming known and engaging with consumers.

5. CAUSE MARKETING

IF YOUR BUSINESS or brand doesn't associate with a cause, consumers may turn to your competitors who do. The number of consumers who say they would switch from one brand to another if the other brand were associated with a good cause has climbed to 87 percent, a dramatic increase in recent years, according to a Cone Cause Evolution Survey.[1]

Blake Andrews and Caroline Pinal were working in the Special Projects Manager for TOMS Shoes to learn about social entrepreneurship and the one-for-one business model pioneered by founder and chief shoe giver of TOMS, Blake Mycoskie.

On a Giving Trip to El Salvador and Nicaragua to give shoes to children in need, Blake fell in love with the people of Nicaragua and decided to dedicate his life to giving back, internationally and domestically. He knew that if a shoe could improve a child's well being then a home could change a child's life.

This light bulb moment lead to the idea of connecting real estate agents with families in need of safe homes. Not long after this spark, Blake launched Giveback Homes in August 2013.

Giveback Homes is a community of real estate professionals who are committed to creating social change by helping build homes for deserving families around the globe. They work together to organize fundraising events, mobilize teams of volunteer homebuilders, and inspire others to take action for social good.

Jessica Northrup is a 23 year real estate veteran and ranks in the top 1% of producing brokers in the Denver area. With each home she sells, she contributes toward building homes for families in need through the Giveback Homes organization. She's doing well by doing good with cause marketing.

---

1. http://bit.ly/2OCupoj

6. CONTENT CURATION

HERE'S A COMMON problem for almost everybody: We don't have enough time to digest the abundance of information available on the topics we're interested in. One of the ways to stand out, especially in a crowded space, is to help your audience cut through information overload by summarizing the most significant content in a quick and easy bite size "content snack." And, perhaps most significantly, you ADD YOUR OWN INSIGHTS AND COMMENTARY INTO THE MIX.

This is a technique called content curation. It's an attractive strategy, because, if you do it , you may have no competition! Curation can also be an effective strategy, if you lack the time or talent to create original content of your own.

So what type of content should you curate?

You'll want to mix it up with local real estate stories and general fun and interesting news from your local area. Publishing these type of stories allows you to be part of the local conversation. That means consistently finding the top trending stories, evolving news, and local developments.

CONTENT CURATION TOOLS

HAVING A TOOL that helps you discover the right content for you to curate is not only a huge time saver, but also a smarter way to deliver more of what your audience wants. Three of my favorite tools for easily finding timely content are:

FEED.LY

FEEDLY IS A must-have in content curation. You can: subscribe to your favorite websites, publications, blogs and YouTube channels, consume the content in a distraction free mode, save it for later, or share it easily on social media. Feedly also allows you to organize your feeds into collections. It's free of charge, but paid version allows log-ins with your team.

POCKET

POCKET IS A great place to get into the habit of accruing content to save and share later. Instead of a laundry list of bookmarks or countless emails you've sent to yourself with links, it keeps all your interesting images, articles, and videos in one place for reference.

BUZZSUMO

BUZZSUMO IS A great tool for uncovering the best content (ranked by shares) published by an individual or a website. Using BuzzSumo, you can type in a domain or keyword and be met with a handful of resources within seconds that are related to those terms or articles published on that domain.

BEST PRACTICES

IT IS IMPORTANT to follow proper etiquette when curating original content from another site. You want to explain to your readers where the information came from and avoid pulling the entire piece verbatim. Small-sized excerpts are fine, but copying an entire article can hurt your rankings on search engines and make your efforts look questionable to site visitors.

- Always link back to the original source of the content. Make that link prominent.

- When you're tweeting, try to mention the Twitter handle of the author in the tweet.

- When you're sharing on Facebook, tag the original author. These tactics will help you gain the respect of the author and your audience.

- Curate from a wide variety of sources. Choose only the posts that will truly resonate with your audience.

- Write a new headline. This is especially important when blogging. You don't want to compete with the original author in search results.

- Add your own commentary or opinion. Tell readers why you liked this piece of content, what you disagree with, or how it helped you. Add context!

- Use quotes sparingly. Sometimes, it's nice to share a quote from a piece of content. Always enclose it in quotation marks to show that it's an actual quote, and keep it short.

- If you are simply sharing content, you do not need to purchase the image associated with the content you're curating, as long as you are sharing a link from the original source.

The only content worth publishing is the content your audience wants to consume. Good content curation means taking relevant information and adding your own commentary or takeaway from the points being made.

As long as you attribute the source and use it to make something worthwhile for your readers, you can expect the original creator to appreciate the increased exposure and your readers to enjoy your perspective on new information.

Once you've established a publication schedule—daily, weekly, or monthly depending on the topic—keep to it. You want your audience to depend on you for consistent, relevant content.

The starting point for getting known lives at the intersection of *space* and *place*. Choosing a niche you enjoy and selecting your preferred strategy for becoming known is the formula for success with your personal brand.

THE KEY INGREDIENT

THERE IS, HOWEVER, one last element required. You may have noticed in the personal branding case studies in this chapter a theme woven into each story. It's content.

Content is the fuel that ignites and sustains your personal brand. If your brand doesn't provide the information people need, when they need it, they will look elsewhere. Content is what attracts people to engage, follow, trust you, and ultimately CHOOSE YOU.

Real estate has traditionally been a sales-driven industry. That's why most agents and lenders aren't doing these marketing strategies—they're more focused on short term sales than they are on brand building and building a following through helpful content.

You might not see results for several months. You might spend a few hundred or a few thousand dollars without seeing anything come from it.

And that's where people give up.

In sales-driven industries like real estate, people don't like investing money in things where they don't see immediate ROI—and brand takes time to build up. Real estate agents and lenders who invest in their brand will significantly outsell their competition.

What kind of content is exactly right for you and your brand?

I've created a free *Disrupt or Die Companion Course* with checklists, bonus videos and resources to help guide you even further along your personal branding journey. To get free access to the *Companion Course*, go to:

DISRUPTORDIEBOOK.COM/COURSE

CHAPTER 7

CONTENT MARKETING

T O BECOME KNOWN, you have to create a way for people to connect and engage with you. Content is what you create that mobilizes your journey on the road to becoming known.

The goal of content marketing is not just content. It's to create an emotional connection with people, over time, that leads to awareness, trust, and loyalty. We will not be loyal to a logo or a blog post, but we can become loyal to a *person*.

Whether you like it or not, every person is now a media company. The tools are easy, free, and everywhere. More importantly, producing content is now the standard for all brands and companies.

Some lenders and agents have defended the need to be online or produce content saying: *"I've been in this business fifteen years and doing fine without being on Facebook or creating online content."*

To them I say: Do you want to be in business for another five years? How about three?

Online content today is the equivalent of the yellow pages thirty years ago. If you weren't in the yellow pages, how did you get found? Word of mouth is a part of it, but ARE YOU A LEGITIMATE BUSINESS IF I CAN'T "LOOK YOU UP?"

WORD OF MOUTH HAS BECOME "WORD OF KEYBOARD."

Your business is 100% referral? Great! What's the first thing a referral will do before they call you? Today, people "look you up" online.

They Google your name, check your Facebook page, and look for online reviews. What will they find? If your online presence is a ghost town, can you be a legitimate business? Are you still active? Are you a part-timer?

> You are being evaluated by your online presence. If you're not producing content, you basically don't exist.

Many agents and lenders struggle with content marketing, saying things like "I don't know what to say" or "I don't have time" or my favorite; "I don't like how I look or sound on video."

News flash...That's how you look and sound!

People are going to find out what you look like! We all struggle with our own self-critique of hearing our own voice and seeing our face in video or in pictures. I understand!

Stick with me here, and you'll discover simple ideas for getting started with content marketing that fits your personality and provides a way to create content that helps you become known so people can "look you up."

WHICH CONTENT IS RIGHT FOR YOU?

I'VE GOT GOOD news for you! Let me take some pressure off, if you're feeling like you need to "be everywhere" and do everything. You don't. If you're just one person, that's unsustainable.

Your success with content marketing and becoming known will not come from dabbling in everything. Your success will come from picking one primary content type and going all in on that one thing.

Publishing consistently is a MUST if your goal is to become

known. The next question is what kind of content will you produce and where will you share it?

FOUR CATEGORIES OF CONTENT

To become known, you need to focus on one of these four types of content:

WRITTEN:

> Blogs are easy and low-cost to start, but the biggest challenge with blogging is they can be time-consuming to sustain. They're a key contributor to search engine ranking success and an excellent way to build thought leadership and loyal followers.

AUDIO:

> A podcast or Alexa Flash Briefing is like a mini radio show hosted online. A study by Edison Research showed more than half the people in the United States have listened to one podcast, and nearly one out of three people listen to at least one podcast every month.[1]

VIDEO:

> It's the next best thing to being in person. Video increases engagement, builds trust, and helps your content show up in peoples' social media feeds. Explainer videos, listing videos, local happenings, and helpful tips are great ways to get started. According to Inman, homes listed with video get four times more inquiries, when compared to homes that were listed without video.

---

1. http://bit.ly/38rakJe

Visual:

Infographics, illustrations, and photographs are ideal if you want to build an audience on Facebook, Instagram, or Pinterest. They drive a lot of social-sharing, and, because real estate is visual, are a critical element to your content strategy.

In Chapter 6, you met agents and lenders having success by focusing on one content type or one social media platform. The key is to focus your efforts, choose the type of content you want to get started with, and get really, really good at that.

WHICH OF THE FOUR CONTENT TYPES SHOULD YOU CHOOSE?

THE MOST IMPORTANT thing is to just get started. Here's three considerations to help you identify your content strategy.

1) FIND THE OPEN SPACE

TAKE A CLOSE look at the content being produced in the real estate industry. Try to get a sense for the uncontested spaces, and see if there's an under-served content opportunity there. Review the list of niches in Chapter 6, pick one and then...go for it!

2) DECIDE WHAT YOU LOVE TO DO

CHOOSING AN UNCONTESTED space is important, but if you don't enjoy creating content or learn to enjoy it, you're going to quit. What do you enjoy doing? Writing? Interviewing people? Taking pictures? Showcasing your local community? Have the heart of a teacher? They key is to align what you enjoy doing with the type of content you'll create.

3) MATCH YOUR CONTENT TO YOUR PERSONALITY STYLE

ARE YOU CAMERA shy and not quite ready to go "all-in" on video? Consider podcasting or creating your own Alexa Flash Briefing. Are you an outgoing extrovert? Video might be just the thing to connect with your audience.

If you're unsure of what might be the best fit for you, start with where you're already spending time. If Facebook is your jam and you're ready to get started with video, start there.

Is Instagram more of your vibe? Start creating Instagram Stories, hyper local community pictures, and unique shots of homes. Have the heart of a teacher? Create a YouTube channel, and create videos about living in your local community, helpful home-buying and selling tips and more.

Only by *doing* will you begin to develop your voice and discover which type of content you enjoy most.

Content marketing works, because when done correctly, it's authentic, useful, and perfectly suited for the internet generation. To succeed with content marketing, it's important to understand what's working and what trends to be aware of.

CONTENT MARKETING TRENDS

GETTING ENGAGEMENT ON social media is always evolving. What worked last year may not be what's working today. Here's the latest Social Media trends in no particular order, to help you succeed with your content marketing strategy.

1) CARE ABOUT YOUR AUDIENCE

IF YOU DON'T show any love to your audience, why would you

expect them to show any love or loyalty to you? The top focus for you should be on being responsive to the people who follow you. After all, social media is all about relationships and engagement isn' it?

Questions on Facebook are ranked second (right behind video) as the content type that gets the most engagement. Not only will asking questions help you increase engagement through more likes and comments, but questions start a conversation with your audience, allowing you to get to know one another on a deeper level.

How do you ask questions that drive engagement? Simply create a post a.ka. "status update" asking your question using Facebook's built-in option to add fun color backgrounds to your status updates so they "pop" in the newsfeed.

You can also use a tool like Canva to create a custom image with text overlay for a more professional look to your questions. People then submit a reply to your question as a comment—showing the Facebook algorithm you've got *real* engagement!

Types of questions your can post include:

- Fill in the blank (e.g. "If I could go anywhere in the world, I'd go to _____")

- Trending topics (e.g. "who are you cheering for in the upcoming finals?")

- DIY questions: (e.g. "what's your favorite paint color for the kitchen")

- Offer a giveaway or contest for "funniest caption to this image"

- "If animals could talk, which would be the most rude?"

- Local community questions: "where's the best local dog park"

- Fun debates like "Beatles or Stones"

Google "100 questions for Facebook status" and you'll have a great list to get you started!

Social media will shift even more toward 1:1 interactions, rather than 1: many broadcasting. Your biggest competitive advantage will be doing the things that don't scale: replying to people, jumping into the comments of all your posts and having meaningful interactions.

Let your audience know that they matter to you, and they will help you grow your brand.

2) IN-THE-MOMENT CONTENT VS HIGHLY-PRODUCED CONTENT

THE RISE OF Stories and short-lived, ephemeral content is capturing the hearts and minds of audiences everywhere. Stories can be both video and images. We're talking Instagram and Facebook Stories. Mark Zuckerberg has said Facebook is moving from an age of Newsfeed only to Newsfeed + Stories.

Currently, Instagram has 500 Million daily Story users, and Stories will also become more prevalent on Facebook.

What does that mean for you?

Well, this means an increased focus on people and humanizing your brand. Think about how you can use video, Stories, and images to connect your audience with the human—maybe even, dare I say, the vulnerable—side of your business.

Unlike posts that last in your feed indefinitely, Instagram Stories have a 24-hour shelf life unless saved to your highlights, making them an excellent tool for providing timely, engaging content for your real estate audience. You can also automatically share your Instagram stories to your Facebook page, engaging your audience there as well.

You can go behind the scenes in your real estate business to show your audience a "day in the life" document taking a listing to market or "the life of a loan." Share what motivates you each day. If your team comes together to sponsor, volunteer or enjoy community events, these are all excellent opportunities to create memorable Instagram Stories and videos.

REAL ESTATE TIPS FOR BUYERS, SELLERS & MORE

SHOWING OFF YOUR real estate expertise will help you produce quality content while demonstrating what your audience can when they choose to work with you.

You can use video and images to document the process to prepare a home for sale, showcase neighborhoods, highlight local attractions, and provide all sorts of other valuable information to your audience.

Here's an example of sharing content either as a video or email; For the title or subject line:

ZILLOW WAS WAY OFF!

"DID YOU KNOW that the CEO of Zillow sold his home for 40% less than the "Zestimate." What's a Zestimate? It's Zillow's estimate of how much a property is worth.

Zillow actually has a disclaimer on their website where you can see exactly how INACCURATE they are. They just make it hard to find.

If you're considering selling your home, (or you're looking at homes on Zillow), I would be happy to send you an accurate quote for your home or one you're considering buying."

BRING CLIENT SUCCESS STORIES TO LIFE

DID YOU HELP a client close on a beautiful, new home that they can't wait to show to the world? Help a first-time homebuyer wade through financing options? Instagram Stories allow you to capture the excitement of client success stories with a real-time reflection on the big day. This can be a great way to show off all that you have to offer for prospects and provide a sense of the happiness that comes with closing the deal on a home.

TechCrunch reports that one in five Instagram Stories shared by a brand receives a Direct Message[2]—allowing you to connect 1:1 with your audience, build engagement and have meaningful conversations. The always-online audiences of today want to be involved, interact, and co-create.

3) VIDEO, VIDEO, VIDEO!

VIDEO? A TREND again? Oh yes. For some, video (both live and uploaded) is nothing new. Agents and lenders who want to get noticed and get results with social media *must* have a video strategy, moving forward, to remain relevant.

Currently, video content comprises more than half of all internet traffic, and, according to Cisco Systems, is predicted by 2020, there will be almost A MILLION MINUTES OF VIDEO PER SECOND crossing the Internet.[3] Cisco adds that, by then, 82% OF ALL CONSUMER WEB TRAFFIC WILL BE VIDEO.

---

2. https://tcrn.ch/2OIQOjH
3. http://bit.ly/2OHpceS

Looking back on 2019, it was an exciting year for video as we saw continued growth on Facebook Live and Instagram's IGTV getting traction. People spend *3x more time* watching live-streamed content than they do watching non-live videos. Live streaming is growing with no signs of slowing down.

BuzzSumo reports that video posts outperform image posts by 73% on Facebook.[4]

According to HubSpot:[5]

- 95% of people have watched an explainer video to learn more about a product or service.

- 81% of people have been convinced to buy a product or service by watching a brand's video.

- 85% of people say they'd like to see more video from brands.

Google adds that 40% of millennials trust YouTube for content. It's no surprise that Animoto's research reveals that 26.4% of professional marketers and 18.5% of small and medium-sized business owners say YouTube will be their main video sharing platform in the next year.

How do you compete against the disrupters and discounters?

It's time to start using video *now*. Build trust with your audience through relevant, hyper-local video content.

People are browsing YouTube, searching Google, and even Facebook, to learn more about an area they are planning to move to. They're looking for agents who have local market knowledge in

---

4. http://bit.ly/2uncXgs
5. http://bit.ly/39tAz29

their community and lenders who can guide them in making the right financial decisions. Will that be you?

4) AUDIO

YOU SHOULDN'T DISCOUNT the notion of creating a branded podcast as a way to provide value to your audience. The Industry Syndicate is "the real estate industry's first media network of podcasts, social media shows & flash briefings." Currently the roster includes 30+ different shows with a focus on collaborating with other like-minded real estate and mortgage professionals through the in-app social feed. You can download their app and listen right from your mobile phone.

Edison Research reveals that roughly 32% of Americans listen to podcasts on a monthly basis, with one-third of Americans age 25-54 doing so. Additionally, 6 million more Americans reported listening to podcasts on a weekly basis in 2019 than did so in 2018; of those that do, 40% of them listen to more than one show.[6]

These podcast statistics show that 22% of Americans listen each week. This is a big jump from 17% last year, and represents 62 million Americans. It's also the largest spike in weekly listenership ever recorded in this study, which dates back to 2013.

Being a real estate professional means you are a *local* business person who knows (or should know) what is happening in your city. People will look to you for information in the real estate arena but also in events, news and everything else local.

Podcasting is a very popular source of information for people. You create an intimate bond with the listener because you are literally talking to them on a daily/weekly/monthly basis.

6. http://bit.ly/2OIwOxC

5) TRANSPARENCY IS KEY

Transparency has become a key focus in the digitally connected era. It's no surprise that with heated online political debates, and the divide over 'fake news', to the controversy over influencer marketing; research indicates consumers are becoming increasingly wary of online claims, and that there's a rising demand for transparency in digital marketing and advertising.

Consumers want more openness, more of a human, social approach, as opposed to businesses simply using social as another broadcast channel for their ads. These are just a handful of the trends we saw emerge in 2019 and believe will continue to shape the digital marketing landscape.

There's no one-size-fits-all marketing strategy, but by keeping these trends in mind when doing your yearly planning, you'll be on the right track.

MAKING TIME FOR CONTENT

Throughout this book, we've shared examples of agents and lenders who have become known in their space through content. They're busy people just like you and me. The real difference between those who succeed with content marketing or not is *choosing* to make it a priority and having the commitment to learning, adapting and staying consistent with it.

I can't help you with your commitment, but I can help you with five ways to fit content marketing into your busy life.

1. Use a content planner. The first and most essential thing you can do is to get yourself organized and implement a system. Plotting out your content using a content planning grid can help you brainstorm, visualize your content and create a workable plan.

2. MAKE TIME TO PLAN AND CREATE. Time-block out several uninterrupted hours each week on your calendar for creating content. This is an appointment with yourself and is a critical part to your success.

3. USE THE TOOLS. Connect your Instagram account to your Facebook page, and you can share Instagram stories directly to your Facebook page. There are apps to help you create content right from your mobile phone or laptop. Videos, images, stories even podcasts can be created on your smartphone now.

4. SCHEDULE CONTENT IN ADVANCE. Having a consistent post schedule is essential, and it is definitely tough in the real estate business. Facebook has its own, built-in scheduling tool allowing you to schedule your posts in advance. Tools like Hootsuite, SproutSocial and others can help you schedule and post your content to social media in advance. However, scheduled content should never replace the personal side of social media which includes natively posting content, engaging and commenting.

5. SCHEDULE SOCIAL TIME: When time blocking to create content, always plan a window of time to respond to comments and engage with others in your community. It's easy to get lost down the rabbit hole of social media platforms. Being intentional with your "on time" of when you'll respond to comments and engage with your audience helps you have purpose, be focused and not waste time watching cat videos.

There's your five steps to making time for content marketing and engaging on social media while still having a life. Use the ideas and you'll be more consistent and feel less overwhelmed with creating content and being on social media.

Of course, hiring a Virtual Assistant or team member to help with scheduling and posting your content can be a huge time saver. Websites like Upwork and Fiverr can be good places to find people at very affordable rates.

PILLAR CONTENT VS MICRO CONTENT

WANT TO SAVE even more time and increase your reach? When you create content—you can repurpose it to give it a longer shelf life.

Pillar content is one substantive and informative piece of content on a specific topic or theme that can be broken into many derivative sections, pieces, and materials. Examples of content pillars include blog posts, eBooks, guides, long form videos (3 minutes or more) Facebook Live videos and podcasts.

Basically, it's a large piece of content that has shelf life and you can turn into many smaller pieces of content like infographics, short form videos, social media updates, and more. By focusing your attention on creating a content pillar, you can re-purpose pillar content into smaller pieces of micro-content that can be shared across many social platforms.

Pillar content is something you consistently post once a week or, at a minimum, several times a month. This could take many different forms—for example, if you're not comfortable on video, you could record a podcast. You might even film yourself recording the podcast so you could get a video out of it as well. And from that video or audio clip, you can create contextual content for Instagram, Twitter, Facebook, LinkedIn, and more.

MICRO CONTENT

MICROCONTENT IS CREATED from your pillar content and is

used to stay top of mind with brand awareness and drive engagement. It typically is something that is eye-catching such as as Instagram or Facebook Stories, graphics, short form videos photos, quotes or it could also be Alexa Flash Briefings.

Microcontent can also be stand-alone, "filler content" in-between your pillar content that may include topics like market updates, "Tuesday Tips," or listings you're promoting on social media.

When repurposing content across different social platforms, don't just 'copy and paste.' Sharing on Instagram would include relevant hashtags and some emoji's or using Stories but that same content on Twitter would be shorter and posted to Facebook be more conversational with comments. Make sense?

Listen to your audience to find out what pieces of pillar content resonated with them, create more content around the key elements that stood out with your audience. Continue this process, refine your approach, and you'll create more relevant content in less time.

Creating content and becoming known is not a 'quick fix.' The agents and lenders that are getting high intent leads from people consuming their content have invested in thoughtful content creation, remained consistent over time, and *personally* engage with their audience.

Not only does content demonstrate knowledge and expertise to potential customers, it's what search engines put in their search results to help people discover you.

Content marketing is just one way to generate leads for your business. Let's get into additional methods of lead generation in the next chapter.

Want more help with content marketing?

Download your free Content Marketing Checklist, bonus videos and resources to help guide you even further along your journey. To get free access to the *Companion Course*, go to:

DISRUPTORDIEBOOK.COM/COURSE

Chapter 8: Lead Generation

Search Google using the phrase "lead generation ideas for real estate," and you'll get over 40,000,000 results back rom Google. That's a lot of ideas!

Today, less than two decades after the arrival of the internet, Google and Facebook together command more advertising dollars than all print media on the planet.

To give us some clarity, let's take a moment and define what lead generation is.

> Lead generation is a way of attracting and warming up potential customers to your business and getting them on the path to eventually choosing you.

The goal of this chapter is to give you the TRUTH about lead generation and what's *really* working today; accumulated from actual conversations with active and productive agents and lenders across North America.

The truth is...

I've met real estate professionals who succeed with door knocking, cold-calling Expired's and FSBO's, geographic farming, direct mail and newspaper advertising.

I've met lenders and agents who get leads *and close deals* from online sources including Zillow, Lending Tree, Nerd Wallet, Facebook Ads, Google Pay-per-Click ads and more.

Every day, agents and lenders also get leads and referrals from their Sphere of Influence, through online content, social media, being active in their local communities and staying top of mind with past clients through database marketing.

In a recent survey posted to industry Facebook groups, agents and lenders responded to the question: "My last transaction came from"...

Here are the bulk of the responses: Past Client & Referral (the majority) Social Media (paid & organic) Door-knocking Yard Sign Direct Mail / Geo-Farming Lender Referral Open House

So there's a lot of options and noise around lead generation.

What *really* works for lead generation in real estate and mortgage? The truth is...it depends.

> Everything works but not everything works equally well all the time. What works in one market may completely fail in another market. What gets results for one person may not be the right activity for someone else.

PRINCIPLES DON'T CHANGE; TACTICS DO!

I DO BELIEVE that certain strategies and principles can be successful in any market, *if* they are applied in the right way.

However, THE WORST NUMBER IN MARKETING IS THE NUMBER ONE. When you rely on just one method to generate leads, you leave your business vulnerable. What happens when that one source diminishes or gets disrupted? Your business and income will suffer.

Our industry has divided into two ways of generating leads. The easy and expensive way and the harder and less expensive way. These are of course 'Buying Leads' vs. 'Generating Leads'.

To have a sustainable business and income, you need to use a combination of leads generated via referrals, content marketing, prospecting and possibly online advertising.

Here are the 6 types of real estate lead sources starting with highest quality:

1. Referrals & Repeat Business

2. Organic (Not paid)

3. Prospecting & Farming

4. Online Portals

5. Google Ads (PPC)

6. Paid Social Media

Typically, the higher the quality of lead source, the lower the quantity of leads, time and effort needed to result in a closed transaction.

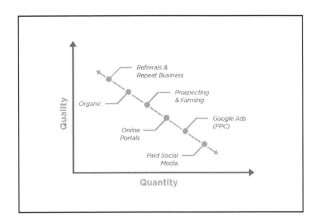

QUALITY VS QUANTITY LEADS

THE FURTHER DOWN the list you go from quality to quantity, the more effort and time required to convert those leads. Sure, you can generate a lot of leads with Facebook ads but the average conversion ranges from 0.5%–3%.

With online leads, you better have your lead contact and follow-up systems on point. In fact, your odds of conversion drop by 400 percent if you wait just 10 minutes to respond to an online lead as reported in the classic Lead Response Management Study.

In this chapter, we'll look at the pros and cons of each of the six lead sources, with actionable plans for how to incorporate them into your lead generation strategy to disrupt proof your business.

Let's start with looking at the primary—yet often overlooked, lead source where the majority of transactions actually come from.

LEAD SOURCE #1: REFERRALS AND REPEAT BUSINESS

IN ITS 2019 Profile of Homebuyers and Sellers Report, the National Association of REALTORS reports that referrals by friends, neighbors, or relatives were higher among younger buyers such as 28 years and younger (52 percent) and 29 to 38 (50 percent) compared to older generations. Look closer at the data and you'll find that 74% of buyers said they would definitely use the same agent they previously worked with but...only 25% actually do! That's a problem.

Lenders, you're in the same boat. Credit reporting agency MonitorBase reviewed public record data and reported only approximately 25% of homeowners use the same lender for their next transaction.

Why does this happen?

I've come to the conclusion that most agents and lenders neglect cultivating a database of past clients for three reasons.

1. It's detailed, mundane work and a good percentage of salespeople are not ideally suited for details and data entry.

2. High performing salespeople get pumped from the thrill of the hunt and winning vs. farming, and tilling the garden.

3. People are easily distracted by "bright shiny object" syndrome.

You've likely heard the statistics that it costs 5x more to acquire a new customer than to keep an existing one. Marketing is becoming more expensive, and getting attention from people is becoming increasingly harder.

> If you want to disrupt proof and grow your business, the first place to invest is your past clients and sphere of influence.

You don't get referrals and repeat business from strangers, you get them from the relationships you have established in life which are the people who know you at some level. These people are your...

SPHERE OF INFLUENCE (SOI)

WHAT'S THE FIRST advice given to new real estate agents and lenders? *START WITH YOUR SPHERE OF INFLUENCE.*

When I began my career as a Loan Originator, my manager told me I needed to write letters, send emails and cards to all the people in my sphere of influence, telling them I was now in the mortgage business. (*This was before Social Media!*)

What sphere of influence? Who are all these people I should be contacting? I didn't influence anyone except possibly my two dogs at home and *only* when I gave them doggie treats!

What exactly is a Sphere of Influence?

A sphere of influence is a list of people comprised of everyone you know and everyone who knows you. This includes past clients, family, friends and people you encounter everywhere you go; including work, kids school, in neighborhoods, clubs and organizations, doing errands, attending parties, and religious affiliations.

There are 5 primary ways to reach and grow your past clients and Sphere of Influence.

- Database marketing
- Client Events
- Get active in your local community (*still works!*)
- Connect and engage on social media

Let's take a closer look at each of the ways to reach your SOI with real-world examples of how you can generate referrals and repeat business.

DATABASE MARKETING

THE AVERAGE HOMEOWNER moves every seven to eight years, according to the latest from ATTOM Data Solutions.

So, if you have 100 people inside your database, you should be getting seven to ten transactions every year from that source. If you're not getting 7-8% of the total number of people inside your database to interact, engage, or choose you, you're not connecting them in a relevant way and you're not getting that business.

What is database marketing? It's the systematic process of staying in touch with your sphere of influence. It means that you have a *plan* and a *system* with repeatable and automated aspects that make it easy to sustain.

People do business with people they know, like, trust, but also...who they REMEMBER!

> The goal of running an effective database marketing campaign is not to generate leads, it's to remain top of mind.

In 2004 Gary Keller published his best-selling book *The Millionaire Real Estate Agent.* He offered The 33 Touch Campaign as a systematized approach to stay in touch with your database over the course of one year. Keller's research indicates that people need to see and hear from you 33 times per year to remember you and for you to stay top of mind.

This is fundamentally still true today. The principle of frequency hasn't changed but tactics have expanded. The rise of social media and technology has provided additional ways to stay top of mind with our past clients and sphere of influence which, we'll explore in this chapter.

But...don't make the mistake of relying solely on technology and automation. It's the human touch, the emotional connection to *you* that keeps people involved and loyal.

There are many variations and methods of database marketing. The following is just one example of a possible modern database marketing strategy.

Database Marketing Example

1. Weekly social media engagement with your past clients and SOI

2. Alexa Flash Briefing featuring local happenings and real estate tips

3. Facebook ads to a *Custom Audience of your SOI (*More on this later*)

4. Send 1-2 *relevant*, monthly emails

5. Make 2–4 phone calls (every 6 months or quarterly)

6. Send 12 relevant direct mailers (once per month)

7. Host new client housewarming parties

8. Host two client appreciation events per year

9. Send weekly handwritten thank you cards to your SOI

10. Send Happy Birthday cards to your clients (and their kids!)

A common excuse I hear from agents and lenders who neglect database marketing is *"I don't know what to send."*

Here's the truth...

- People don't care how many houses you sold this month

- People don't want your "turn back the clock" emails

- People don't want to get blasted with your listings and sold's

People generally don't want to talk about real estate until they are in the market to buy or sell or have a *reason* to be interested.

People's interest in real estate can be triggered by market conditions, life events or personal desires like staying informed about their home's financial position or referring you to someone they know.

Jared Hamilton is a Loan Officer with Cherry Creek Mortgage in Denver, CO. He's staying top of mind with his past clients by conducting annual mortgage reviews. He's also creating engagement opportunities using a software called Homebot.ai.

Homebot is the winner of the 2018 Realogy Innovator of the Year Award. It helps home owners save money and build wealth through home ownership.

Homebot drives repeat and referral business for real estate agents and loan officers through "engagement triggers." Clients get a custom branded, personalized monthly digest featuring their property value, equity position, net worth, current loan balance and other helpful information. Not sure if your featured property value is correct? Just tap a button on your mobile phone to send a CMA request direct to the agent and lender.

Sales Boomerang is an automated digital service that gleans data from multiple databases and pings you when life events happen in the lives of your clients—when they're looking to move, when they have a baby, when their credit score is pulled or reaches an important threshold; even when anyone in your database is shopping for a loan.

To be efficient at capturing repeat and referral business, you need a Customer Relationship Database or CRM.

Pick out what you think is the best system and then use it. Add every single contact you have into that system. Then, add notes for each person: like how you met them, their family size, names, if they bought/sold with you, etc. This step is very important, because when you speak with them later on, you can reference those key moments and will be able to build rapport. *People love being remembered!*

Your role today must be as a trusted advisor for your clients vs just selling property or quoting interest rates. The point is to remain connected, keeping the emotional bond and value exchange alive so when they are considering buying or selling, you're the obvious choice. Sending banana bread recipes isn't going to get you there.

CLIENT EVENTS

CLIENT APPRECIATION EVENTS are a proven way to keep the emotional bond alive with past clients, grow your SOI, gain referrals and repeat business.

Josh Anderson is the owner of The Anderson Group Real Estate Services in Nashville and is ranked among the Top 1,000 Real Estate Agents in North America by the Wall Street Journal.

His team sells over 250 homes a year with 70% coming from past clients and SOI. How does he get so much referral and repeat business? Every year, Josh and his team host 5-6 events including client appreciation events and house warming parties.

He's a business savvy professional with a strong desire to cater to his clients' particular needs, hosting events people are actually interested in attending. His plan is simple. He calls and asks clients which kind of event they would be more likely to attend.

What Josh has discovered by engaging clients in a conversation is if your clients are married and have young children, a catered house warming event at home can work much better than after-work drinks.

Josh says "we're doing more family friendly types of events and every time we do it we get referrals out of it. Hosting events helps us get referrals when it caters to the client and when it's something they look forward to attending."

How else do you stay top of mind with your sphere if influence *without* talking about listings, interest rates and open houses all the time? Put yourself in the middle of what people are actually interested in. For most, that's where they live, work and play; in their local community.

POP BY'S

KAREN PETERS HEADS up the #1 Group in Sales for The Coldwell Banker Residential Brokerage in Wayne, NJ. What she's focused on right now is her past clients helping to drive the future of her business.

Every month, her team picks out 30-40 past clients and drops off a gift at their house. "It's a great way to say hello, show them some appreciation and hopefully get that next listing or referral" says Karen.

GET ACTIVE IN YOUR LOCAL COMMUNITY

BEING ACTIVE IN your community is another proven way to stay top of mind with your past clients, expand your Sphere of Influence, and build your database.

Not only will being active in your local community grow your personal brand (as we saw in Chapter 6) and your client base, it will strengthen your knowledge of the neighborhoods you serve and foster a personal connection with the people who live in them.

At the Inman Connect Conference in the summer of 2016, social media marketing leader Gary Vaynerchuk coined the phrase; "become the digital mayor of your town."

Becoming the "digital mayor" means establishing yourself as a reputable, knowledgeable, local market authority and source of relevant community news. Doing so increases the likelihood for buyers to contact you and for sellers to think of you when it's time to sell their homes.

Mayors know a lot about their communities. From investing in the success of local businesses to following high school football rivalries or knowing where to get the best steak dinner, mayors should fully understand and appreciate living in their communities.

Alex Wang, a real estate agent in the Silicon Valley was in the audience when Gary Vaynerchuk espoused the idea of becoming your town's "digital mayor." Alex got to work and hired a videographer to follow him for a year and chronicle the daily life of a real estate agent and report on topical news in his local community.

Alex experienced firsthand how regular community interaction, combined with social media presence will go far in helping create awareness and stay top-of-mind. In 2019, Alex closed 56 transactions; *half* of which was generated from people engaging with him through his online content.

Alex believes that a well-developed personal brand and regular community interaction on social media will go far in helping you stay top-of-mind with clients.

The ideal strategy is to blend the online with offline, to reach more people and grow your personal brand awareness where people live...in your local community.

Agents and lenders can team up to boost their sphere of influence in their local community in a myriad of ways which will generate leads and referrals. Here are a few ideas:

- SEASONAL ACTIVITIES: Kris Lindahl and his brokerage in Minnesota host the annual "Great Pumpkin Giveaway" with over 13,000 pumpkins, live music from The Teddy Bear Band, bounce houses, food trucks, face painting, and so much more! It's a free community event that draws over 1,000 families.

- CAUSE MARKETING: Amber Uhren; Broker/Owner of Realty Billings in Montana's hosts the annual "Socktober" drive. Each year they enlist the help of hundreds of local businesses, schools and residents to help fill the Realty Billings branded truck with donations of over 7,000 pairs of new socks, helping local homeless organizations.

- LOCAL EVENTS: Annemarie de Lebohn with TNG Real Estate in Southern California hosts two free "Shred Events." The events reduces paper in the landfill and helps people reduce identity theft. Agents farm neighborhoods with flyers, door hangers and get active on social media, informing people they can shred up to five boxes of paper for free, which is about a $100 savings.

- PET ADOPTION DAY: People love their pets—most people consider them members of the family. Alisa Cunningham with Doulas Elliman partners with local animal shelters or rescue groups to sponsor a pet adoption event. You pay for renting a space, tables and canopy shelters, maybe hire food trucks, promote it on social media, your SOI and then show up and work the event.

Okay, I know what you're thinking. Getting people off Netflix and out of the house is super hard. While that may be true, it's much easier to promote events *you* care about. The key is to try and plan events around your own passions and hobbies. Here are some additional ideas you can try:

- Organize a tour of a local historic neighborhood
- Set up a wine or beer tasting at a local micro brewery
- Host an end of season party for your local youth soccer team
- Run an educational seminar on a real estate investing
- Charter a fishing or whale watching boat
- Organize a cleanup day at a local park or beach for charity
- Hire a local interior designer or professional organizer and host a class
- Hold informational seminars or mixers for first time buyers
- Rent out a local theater and host a film showing
- Organize a kickball game and provide a box lunch & drinks
- Coordinate a day hike for local families

Even with the continued intrusion from technology, real estate is still a people business. As we saw in Chapter 6, getting involved in charitable causes like Give Back Homes or others may help you gain new customers since many people have charitable causes they are passionate about and people prefer to do business with brands associated with a cause.

CONNECT AND ENGAGE ON SOCIAL MEDIA

BEFORE SOCIAL MEDIA, to be active in your community meant in person only. Today, you can combine the offline with online for a powerful two punch combo that can help scale your reach and expand your Sphere of Influence.

Being a real estate agent professional means you're a local expert doesn't it? Consider creating a Facebook Community Page or Group featuring local content and topics of interest for people who live in the community.

Karen Migos with Towne Realty Group runs a Facebook Group with over 5,000 members called: *365 Things To Do In Millburn & Short Hills, NJ*. She shares what's happening in Millburn Township, "a great town to visit, shop, dine, play, learn & a place to be home."

Kyle Whissel with EXP Realty and his team are ranked as the #1 real estate team in San Diego and #76 team in the U.S. by The Wall Street Journal. His Facebook Page; *Everything East County* is a place where you can stay informed and talk about everything going on in East County San Diego.

Kyle recommends creating a separate Facebook page or group for your community content. He had another Facebook page that he ran for two years where he talked about food, fitness, and fashion, but because he published the content on his real estate page, he saw far less engagement and after several years, never grew beyond 6,000 followers.

Kyle added; "people don't want to like a real estate page unless they're interested in real estate. If you're going to make content about food, fashion, fitness, or local happenings, put it on a separate page. You'll be shocked how many people like that page versus your real estate page." With the change in strategy, Kyle saw his followers and engagement grow from a plateau of 6,000 followers to over 20,000 page followers.

Connecting with past clients and your local community, both in person and on social media, is an important element of modern marketing strategy. Agents and lenders who create content with a focus on hyper-local and consistently remain top of mind with their Sphere of Influence will face less threats of disruption than those who don't.

LEAD SOURCE #2: ORGANIC LEADS

THE TERM "ORGANIC leads" is often associated with people finding you through a Google search rather than clicking on an ad.

Your online audience and your local community can be considered a source of organic leads also. When a stranger or someone within your sphere of influence initiates a conversation with you by showing an organic interest in your business, the transition from stranger to customer is a much more natural, organic (vs paid ad) process.

Where do you find organic leads? You don't find them. They find you just like they found Alex Wang in Silicon Valley when he took hold of the "digital mayor" concept.

You can generate organic leads through sharing relevant content on social platforms, your website, or blog. Anyone who sees your content without you having to pay for people to see it is a potential organic lead or referral source. They are your *audience* of people who get to know you, trust you, and like you, even if they've never done business with you.

Alex McFadyen started his Mortgage Brokering business from scratch in 2015 with a simple mission. "My goal is to be the most recommended broker in the industry, through providing customers with trustworthy advice, personal service, and an exceptional experience."

His consistent presence and brand awareness helped him quickly grow his business to close over 300 loans in 2019.

How did he grow so quickly? Alex knew that first time homebuyers find the process of obtaining a mortgage daunting and confusing. He took to social media with a focus on educating through video content and having fun vs selling.

His "Learn With the Mortgage Pug" #mortgagepug series of videos educates people about buying, refinancing, market updates and more with the assistance of his amazing sidekick Ernie the pug.

Early on, the audience for Alex's videos was his own sphere of influence. With consistency in posting videos, came exponential growth. His videos improved, and his engagement with his sphere grew deeper. He demonstrated his knowledge through helpful and fun content, and his audience began sharing his videos, sending referrals, and igniting his business—*organically.*

You can hear Alex share his story on the Mortgage Marketing Radio Podcast Episode #118. Listen here: www.MortgageMarketingInstitute.com/118

COMMUNITY PAGES ON YOUR WEBSITE

PERHAPS ONE OF the most overlooked ways to generate organic leads is to start your own page on your website for your local area or various neighborhoods.

The majority of people begin their search online. The advantage to a webpage or website full of quality, hyper local content, is you showing up and ranking high in Google searches.

When home buyers begin their online search for a new place to live, they first want to know more about where they will potentially move. Most people search for locally focused keywords such as the name of towns or counties, local school districts, or housing prices in your area.

A community page provides the perfect platform to rank highly for all these search terms. Here you can address common questions about the region and establish yourself as a helpful resource, just as potential leads are beginning their home buying or selling journey.

On her website, agent Deborah Hess of The Chicago Group provides detailed information about each area of the city where she helps people buy and sell homes. Her page about living in Logan Square, for example, takes a deep dive into the neighborhood, facts about the community's history, architecture, quality photos, home prices, transportation and popular hangouts that actually makes people feel like they're there.

RE/MAX on the River in Massachusetts was named an "Up & Comer" by Real Trends for having over 600 transactions in 2019! Their community page videos don't just provide viewers with a rundown of the community; they also feature the brokerage's agents where each employee shares their own favorite place to visit, or local activity such as apple picking.

Not only can viewers get an idea of what it's like to live in the area; they also get familiar with each agent, paving the way for a strong agent-client relationship in the future.

> Organic leads are higher quality because you've often earned their trust before they even reach out to you.

"I've been following you for months. We're ready to sell/buy in July and would like to set an appointment with you."

These are the kinds of comments that come from organic leads who've engaged with your content. You don't have to sell them on your services. They're already sold!

Organic lead generation can take a while to get established. It's a good idea to supplement it with other lead generation strategies while you get it going. Let's look at additional ways you can generate leads.

LEAD SOURCE #3: PROSPECTING AND FARMING

PROSPECTING AND FARMING is a mix of sourcing leads, leveraging your social network to create business, and engaging in your community to boost your brand's visibility as discussed earlier.

Real Estate trainer and coach Tom Ferry conducted a study of 3,000 real estate agents and discovered that of those surveyed, agents who prospect five or more hours a week made more than $200,000 a year.

Tim Smith is the leader of Coldwell Banker's #1 Team in California with over $2 billion in sales. He measures his team's day-today prospecting success by two metrics that should be familiar to anyone in sales: appointments and contracts.

He calls it his 5-5-4 routine. Every day, you should have:

- 5 Conversations with new potential prospects (people you don't know)
  *Yes, Tim still cold calls for listings!

- 5 Conversations with your hottest prospects (follow-up calls)

- 4 Conversations with your Sphere of Influence

THE KEY TO THIS SYSTEM IS *CONVERSATIONS*. It could take you 25 calls to have five conversations with your SOI.

Tim's two "golden questions" he asks on calls are: *"have you had any thoughts of selling?"* and *"do you know anyone who's had thoughts of selling?"*

Some people think of prospecting and farming as "old school" activities including phone calls, postcards and flyers or door knocking. Some people will say those methods no longer work or are dying. I prefer to look at actual results vs. opinions.

California REALTOR® Ramon Sanchez has been in real estate over twenty five years and credits prospecting Expired listings as a key contributor to his growth. Ramon will be the first to admit that making cold calls isn't easy, but prospecting produced the majority of his 41 closed transactions for gross commissions earned of $544,235.00. So despite hearing "no" day after day, Ramon definitely isn't putting down the phone anytime soon.

Are FSBO's your jam? There are plenty of places to get local FSBO leads including Zillow's "Make me Move" or FSBO listings. Want FSBO leads delivered to your inbox? REDX and

LandVoice are lead generation services that search FSBO listings across multiple sources the day they hit the market and deliver them to your inbox.

What about geo-farming a specific area? Done correctly, geographic farming can still be an effective way to grow and maintain a successful real estate business. Many agents however waste too much time engaging people who can't or won't sell a home anytime soon.

Predictive analytics companies, like SmartZip, Remine and Revaluate, make it possible for agents and lenders to target and reach out only to someone who is likely to move based on big data and artificial intelligence.

Think getting listings from postcard mailers doesn't work?

Daniel Beer is the CEO/Owner of Beer Home Team of eXp Realty of California, Inc., one of the Top 150 Teams in the nation per *The Wall Street Journal.* Dan's #1 source of business is geo-farming with postcards. In 2018 Dan and his team sold 303 homes in San Diego earning $4.5+ million GCI.

Robin Mann, REALTOR® in Charlotte, NC is passionate about door knocking. Door-knocking doesn't need to be sleazy or awkward—it can be a great way to network in a neighborhood, drum up new contacts and invite prospective buyers to open houses.

She believes door knocking is all about mindset. She takes notes on her phone from conversations with homeowners during her door knocking and sends thank you cards and when needed, retrieves the homeowners name from the county tax records when.

While door knocking her farm, she noticed one homeowner answering the door with her arm in a sling. Robin expressed her empathy and followed up by sending the homeowner a "get well soon" card. Four months later, that homeowner contacted Robin and sold her house.

Her second year as an agent, Robin sold 26 homes, mostly from door knocking. Her third year, she integrated community pages and Facebook groups into her marketing mix, selling 56 homes.

NOT ONE SIZE FITS ALL

EARLIER IN THIS chapter I said: "what gets results for one person may not be the right activity for someone else and what works in one area may not work in another."

The 5-5-4 plan works for Tim Smith and his team. Cold-calling Expired's works for Ramon in his area, and it works for many other agents too. Geo-farming with postcards works for Dan Beer, and door knocking works Robin Mann. You'll have to decide which prospecting activities are right for you and your local area. Remember, the goal of prospecting and lead generation is ultimately to DRIVE CONVERSATIONS with people that lead to loan applications, purchase contracts and closed transactions.

> There is no such thing as ONE way to grow your mortgage or real estate business. Remember, principles don't change; tactics do.

While traditional prospecting has its appropriate place, with today's technology, you can potentially reach thousands of people within minutes online and narrow your focus to a specific geographic radius to enhance your prospecting and farming strategy. We'll unpack how to do that when we review lead generation tactic #6, Paid Social Media.

Let's look at the next source of leads; online portals.

LEAD SOURCE #4: ONLINE PORTALS

THE PORTALS ARE giant home search websites from which you can buy leads. Due to their vast resources, they rank high for the most competitive keywords on Google. Portal sites include Zillow, Trulia, Realtor.com, Homes.com, and they garner the lions share of traffic and visitors from people searching for homes online.

Traffic to Zillow Group's mobile apps and websites reached an all-time high in the third quarter of 2019 with average monthly unique users up 5% year over year to 195.6 million. Website visits for 2019 exceeded 2.1 billion, up 11% year over year.

Zillow's Premier Agent program, the largest online lead portal, was re-vamped in 2018 and since then, many agents note significant improvements in its program and lead quality. Zillow reported third quarter 2019 growth of 7% from its Premier Agent business.

The sustainability of Zillow's Premier Agent program is foundational to Zillow's success in expanding its Zillow Offers program.

Our intent is not to debate Zillow but to evaluate the ability to profitably generate leads from Zillow and other online portals if you choose to invest. On one topic about Zillow, there is no debate. During at least one point in their home search, most buyers visit Zillow.

Lenders, Zillow is now your competition since they entered the mortgage business. I've spoken with many lenders who are co-paying with agents for Zillow leads. Evaluating your ROI and return on that agent relationship is critical.

Some lenders feel beholden to keep co-paying for Zillow leads with agents out of fear they'll lose out on the agents other business.

My advice for lenders is to be vigilant as Zillow rolls out plans to take a bigger bite out of the mortgage pie.

Zillow's five year origination forecast would place them as a top 20 national lender. For comparison, Quicken Loans has a market share of six percent, after 35 years of being exclusively focused on lending.

If you're overly dependent on Zillow co-paid leads with agents, it's time to re-evaluate those relationships and potentially diversify your lead sources.

You can bet Zillow will be utilizing their vast resources to deliver a single source to consumers of finding a home and delivering the mortgage. It's time to get to the customer first with your content marketing, past client activities and other lead sources...NOW!

Agents, it's time to stop complaining about getting "ripped off by Zillow"—starting with a frank conversation on what it really takes to win with online portal leads, and look at it from a cost vs benefit analysis.

Most agents are way too shortsighted when it comes to converting leads. They get impatient if the lead doesn't demand to start making offers on homes on day one. That's like going fishing and getting frustrated that the fish aren't jumping into the boat!

Dig deeper into the person's business who's complaining about paid leads not converting, and often you'll find that there are critical elements missing from that person's overall business systems.

TO SUCCEED WITH PAID, ONLINE LEADS YOU MUST HAVE FOUR THINGS:

1. Proper mindset and understanding of online leads

2. Adequate and sustainable budget

3. Professional online presence

4. Lead management policy and conversion process

The pro of purchasing real estate leads from online portals is they can give you some immediate action in your pipeline. Many of those leads have higher intent and are further along in their timeline for buying or selling compared to leads from places like Craigslist and Facebook ads.

For hot leads coming in from portals like Zillow, fast response times are crucial. A fast, automatic and *personal* response for these hot leads is critical to your conversion rate, especially when you consider how many other agents may be contacting them.

Long-term lead nurture strategies are the fundamental difference between moving from a 1% conversion on leads to upwards of 5% conversion rates. A great CRM will help you build and maintain a real connection with thousands of leads, without having to sacrifice your personal life or having to guess which leads actually want to hear from you.

HOW TO CALCULATE YOUR ROI ON PAID LEADS

ONE WAY TO calculate the profitability of paid leads is to divide your Gross Commission Income (GCI) by lead cost.

Joe Schwartzbauer of Grey Duck & BRIX Real Estate in St. Paul Minnesota; achieves an 8% lead conversion rate from Zillow Premier Agent leads. In 2019 he invested $21k into Zillow and closed $88k in commissions. That's a 4X Return on lead cost.

Joe does well with Zillow leads, because he has the four elements required, we mentioned above.

He leverages his CRM to segment Zillow leads by timeline to purchase a home. Based on lead stage, Joe's CRM sends the appropriate drip campaigns, sets tasks for calls, sends video messages, automated texts and emails at different frequencies.

Your lead costs from online portals may vary based on your location, average home prices (since the expected GCI is higher) how many other agents are competing for leads in your zip code and your total budget for leads. How much you spend and the quality of the leads coming in are all important parts of setting a profitable strategy for working your paid leads.

There are the five steps to getting the best ROI from online lead portals.

1) Pick the Right Zip Code

When picking a ZIP code, first consider how familiar you are with the area. Knowing the neighborhood gives you authority, helps clients trust you, and ensures more referrals. Next, consider ZIP codes with less competition and low home prices; this ensures the leads will be less expensive. Finally, consider areas next to ZIP codes with high home sale prices as proximity to these areas is desirable.

2) Create a Professional Agent Profile

Upload a professional headshot, a bio highlighting your expertise in the local area, and perhaps a well-crafted intro video. If you volunteer at local organizations or have a particular specialty as an agent, this is the area to discuss it. Be sure to include reviews from happy former clients and a direct link to your website.

3) Reach Out to Past Clients for Reviews

For agents, having multiple five-star ratings on your Zillow Premier Agent helps establish trust and credibility. To ensure a strong rating, identify five to 10 former clients who had great experiences working with you, and personally contact them to ask for a review.

4) Follow Up With Leads Immediately

You can set up an autoresponder using Zillow's free Premier Agent app. It's also a good idea to send a more personalized message (think video) like Joe Schwartzbauer does. With the increase in automated responses from real estate agents, consumers value a personal touch.

Another option is to use a third-party CRM programs like BoomTown, Property Base, Wise Agent, Lion Desk, Ylopo and others.

5) Nurture Leads Through the Sales Process

While Online Portal leads often have higher intent to buy or sell than Facebook lead ads, most will not be ready for six months or longer. You're going to have to communicate with them regularly until they're ready to buy or sell with relevant content including market updates, new listings, community information and client success stories. Having a good CRM helps you manage the lead nurturing process.

LEAD SOURCE #5: GOOGLE ADS (PPC)

PAY-PER-CLICK ADVERTISING (PPC) is a well-established form of online marketing that aims to drive targeted web traffic to an advertiser's website.

Basically, anytime you are doing a search on a search engine like Google or looking at the pages of another website you'll see advertisements on those search results or web pages.

Google actually has two different "networks" to run ads on.

1) Display Network

The Google Display Network is the set of third-party websites that have agreed to show Google ads on their website pages. Have you ever noticed certain ads seem to "follow you" around the web as you visit different websites? This is an example of an advertiser using the Google Display Network to show their ad to you as you browse the web.

Display ads will show up as you browse the web based on the targeting options the advertiser has chosen. For example:

- Keywords and topics related to what the advertiser offers
- Specific websites or pages you visit
- Specific audiences based on interests or demographics

Generally speaking, Display ads are designed to target buyers early in the sales cycle, because the people browsing the web aren't actively searching for a product and likely haven't yet entered keywords and terms into a Google search.

2) Search Network

When you think of Google Ads, you're probably thinking of search ads.

These are the ones that appear next to the search results as people enter keywords into a Google search for related products or services.

Search ads are triggered by keywords; if a user's search query matches one of your keywords, your ad could appear above or alongside the search results.

Google's search network is where Pay-per-Click (PPC) ads

appear, above, below the organic search results and on the right side of the Google search page. As its name implies, PPC ads are priced on a cost-per-click (CPC) basis, meaning the advertiser is charged a small amount every time somebody clicks on an ad.

The basic Pay-Per-Click (PPC) formula is:

Pay-per-click ($)

=

Total Advertising Spend ($)

÷

Number of Ads clicked.

The average cost-per-click for the real estate industry is $0.75 on the Display Network and $2.37 on the Search Network. (Word-Stream 2018)

Your cost-per-click is calculated on the fly every time your ad appears, according to a process known as the ad auction. The ad auction is Google's way of deciding which ads to display when someone performs a keyword search, what order to rank the ads in, and how much each online advertiser pays per click.

For specific cost-per-click estimates, use Google's Keyword Planner Tool and Bid Simulator. These free tools from Google will help give you an idea of how much your costs per click will be.

CLICK-THROUGH-RATE

ANOTHER METRIC IS the click-through-rate (CTR), which is defined as the number of clicks made on your ad (click-throughs), divided by the total number of *impressions* (number of times that your ad is shown):

Click-through rate (%) = (Total Number of Ad Clicks ÷ Total Number of Ad Impressions) x 100

Click-through rate is expressed as a percentage so for ease of use, x 100 is added to the above equation.

As an example, if 100 people saw your ad and 10 people clicked on your ad, then your click-through-rate would be 10%. That would be amazing of course!

Advertising on Google Ads is not the same as on Facebook. On Facebook, you advertise primarily based on interests and Custom Audiences. More on that in a moment. On Google, however, you can target based on intent.

WHAT DO I MEAN BY INTENT?

WHEN PEOPLE DO a Google search for terms like:

"Akron OH Homes for Sale" "Las Vegas Homes for Sale" "Homes for Sale in Highlands Ranch CO" "How Much House Can I Afford"

These people have a higher INTENTION or likelihood for being ready to buy, based on the keywords they've entered into a Google search.

With keywords, you can target based on where a lead is in the buying or selling process and get hyper local to your area. Google Search Ads are best used for higher intent leads because users are actively searching keyword terms.

Do you specialize in specific areas or neighborhoods? You'll want to take advantage of the geographical targeting that Google provides you. You can break your targeting down to only show ads in specific zip codes, getting hyper local with your lead generation.

KEYWORD RESEARCH

WANT TO SEE how many people are searching for *your* key-words?

Knowing the search volume, potential clicks and cost-per-click for your keywords can make or break your success with online ads. You'll also learn a lot about what people are searching for which can be helpful with your content marketing strategy.

Sample Keyword Search Results:

Akron OH Homes for Sale: 1,300 searches per month Las Vegas Homes for Sale: 14,800 searches per month Homes for Sale in Highlands Ranch: 1,600 searches per month How Much House Can I Afford in Texas: 1,300 searches per month

Simply replace the words above with your local area to get results relevant for you.

Here are some free keyword tools to help kickstart your keyword research.

1. Google Keyword Planner

2. Google Trends

3. Keywords Everywhere

4. Ubersuggest

5. Soovle

Are you ready to take advantage of these free keyword tools to produce quality, ads and useful content for your brand? Keyword research is about more than just finding keywords. It's about understanding who is searching for them and *what they want to see.*

CONVERSION RATE

THE CONVERSION RATE of an ad is the percentage of people who, after clicking on an ad, complete an action. What is the action you want from people clicking on your ad? It could be to fill out a contact form, send you a text message or book an appointment. In the context of advertising to generate leads, in most cases it would be to submit their information via a lead capture form or landing page.

Your prospects are not going to buy or sell homes right away after visiting a landing page. So, your focus will obviously be on collecting emails of home buyers and sellers and then launching a drip email campaign to nurture these leads.

So for our purposes, we'll look at the conversion rate for someone seeing your ad, clicking the ad and completing a lead capture form on your website or landing page.

The average conversion rate for the real estate industry is 0.08% on the Google Display Network and 2.47% on the Google Search Network. (WordStream 2018)

That means if 100 people searching Google click your ad, the average number of people who will complete your lead form on your website is 2. Get 500 people to click your ad and approximately 12 people will complete your lead form.

What if 12 people a day completed your lead form? That's 360 "high intent" leads per month! You don't need thousands of leads to succeed when your attracting people further along in their buying or selling journey.

HOW DO YOU IMPROVE CONVERSIONS?

1) A STRONG HEADLINE
Your real estate landing page's headline is the first (and some-

times only) thing that visitors will read from start to finish, so a clear message that captures attention and is easy to understand is a must.

2) A PROFESSIONAL IMAGE
Great landing pages use strong imagery to reinforce (and not distract from) their message. For instance, if you're offering a list of homes in a certain area and price range, your image should represent homes that match the target market.

3) LESS IS MORE
Because they have such a targeted purpose, real estate landing pages generally only have short, direct copy, minimal images and don't ask the user for a lot of information.

According to a study by Wordstream, top of the funnel lead conversions will drop significantly if a landing page has more than four fields to complete. So, stick with only the information you absolutely *need* to deliver the promise of your offer.

4) MOBILE FIRST
Mobile accounts for approximately half of web traffic worldwide. Mobile users on Social Media are even higher. Make sure the mobile experience of your landing page and website is a good one. After creating your landing pages, visit it on your mobile device to make sure the process is smooth and looks as good as it does on desktop.

5) DELIVER ON YOUR PROMISE
Does your landing page deliver on the promise of your ad? Remember, the visitors to this page are coming here seeking answers to a particular question or get information. Don't make the mistake of sending people to your homepage.

If you send a lead right to your homepage, they may click

around, get distracted by something, and never come back. This is not the time to show off your fancy website or video collection. Give the people what they came for. Your prospects will feed betrayed if you don't deliver on your ad promise when they arrive at your home page.

THE 3 TYPES OF LANDING PAGES

1) Home Search

LEAD TYPE:
Buyer

CONVERSION RATE:
Low

BENEFITS:
Higher click-through rate

DRAWBACKS:
Lower conversion rate; people will search for listings on your site but may not sign up

Home search landing pages generate buyer leads by offering a free listing search to those who click on your ad. Leads are then directed to your IDX website so they can search for homes and save their favorites. Typically, after a few minutes of searching, they're encouraged to leave their contact information to continue using the site and receive email updates of new listings.

2) Home Values

LEAD TYPE:
Seller leads

CONVERSION RATE:
Medium to high

BENEFITS:
Can have a good conversion rate

DRAWBACKS:
Can require a subscription to instant home value services

Home value landing pages are among the most popular methods used to get seller leads. Generally speaking, the ad will offer them a free home valuation so they can find out how much their home is worth in today's market. When a potential lead clicks on the ad, they'll be directed to a home value landing page. Obviously you'll need their address and contact information to produce the valuation.

3) Free Content (For Lenders Too)

LEAD TYPE:
Seller or buyer

CONVERSION RATE:
Medium to high

BENEFITS:
Leads will be more likely to leave contact information

DRAWBACKS:
Leads may be further away from making a buying or selling decision

Free content landing pages offer potential leads free content in exchange for their contact information. In the world of digital marketing, this is known as a lead magnet.

Examples of effective lead magnets may be something like a buyer or seller e-book, a guide to off-market listings in your farm area, a list of the top 10 renovations with the best return on investment (ROI), an updated list of foreclosures, how to buy a home with less than 20% down or any other content a buyer or seller might want from a mortgage or real estate professional.

Your landing pages have one purpose; to get people to give you their contact information. Successful landing pages look professional and offer potential leads something of value in exchange for their contact information.

LANDING PAGE TEMPLATES

INSTEAD OF TRYING to reinvent the wheel, just customize one of the hundreds of landing page templates available through services like LeadPops, Empower Funnels, LeadPages, Unbounce, Cloud Attract and many others.

Above is an example of a lead capture page from LeadPops, offering a way for people to see how much home they can qualify for.

Many companies including Placester, BoomTown, Commisions Inc (CINC), offer a complete, all in-one real estate platform that includes Google PPC, landing pages, IDX websites, email, lead nurturing and more.

CAN GOOGLE ADS WORK FOR YOU?

MORTGAGE ORIGINATOR BRENT VanderGriend, in Sioux Falls South Dakota was looking for a way to get to the customer early on Google. He engaged the services of Michael McCallister and Empower Funnels to help him run Pay-per-Click ads on Google.

Over an 18-month period, Brent generated over 5,000 leads and closed nearly 80 loans from Google leads. He also has a pipeline of pre-approved borrowers that he can roll out to his key agent partners. getting to the customer early in their home-buying journey.

LEAD SOURCE #6: PAID SOCIAL MEDIA

FACEBOOK'S ADVERTISING PLATFORM is by the far the most developed of all of the social media platforms. For that reason, our focus for paid social media will be on Facebook.

Instagram is owned by Facebook, so it has access to the same extensive user base and uses the same advertising platform as Facebook and generally follows the same best practices when running paid ads.

The average consumer logs into Facebook 12.2 times per day, and 85% of homeowners are on the platform, making Facebook a rich source of people who may be your next client or referral.

In 2018, after lawsuits from housing groups such as the American Civil Liberties Union and the National Fair Housing Alliance (NFHA), Facebook reached a settlement to make changes that will prevent landlords, employers, lenders, real estate professionals and others from discriminating against these protected classes.

Facebook has since announced Housing as a new ad category and policies specifically geared towards advertisers in housing:

- Facebook will disable targeting that appears to exclude users on the basis of race, gender, age, class, sexual orientation, or religion.

- Facebook's income level and net worth targeting, are discontinued.

- Facebook now requires geo-targeted ads to include a minimum 15-mile radius area to prevent regional discrimination.

- Lookalike audiences are no longer available.

- Facebook is building a tool that will enable users to view all the housing-related ads that are currently running in the US. *Google Facebook Ad Library for more details.

Now when you log into your Facebook ads manager, you'll see Facebook has created a separate advertising portal just for housing, employment, and credit ads. All ads in those categories must be created via the new portal ad are considered a special ad category.

Furthermore, all demographic and behavior targeting options are gone. For example: "newlyweds" "divorced" "empty nesters" "new baby" are now gone.

Facebook has also removed access to any saved audiences. This is designed to prevent the use of any previously created audiences that may include discriminatory targeting.

Facebook no longer allows for the creation of a specific type of Custom Audience known as "look-a-like audiences," as they utilize demographic data of a businesses current customers, website visitors, etc. to identify similar audiences, effectively discriminating against certain people based on demographics.

NOT ALL IS LOST!

FACEBOOK HAS UNVEILED a slightly different custom audience for Special Ad Categories called..."Special Ad Audiences" (creative, huh?).

This "Special Ad Audience" operates in the same fashion as look-a-likes, only instead of using demographic data to build similar audiences, they utilize interest behavior. Essentially, Facebook analyzes current customer interests and internet browsing patterns to identify individuals with similar interests and behaviors to target.

So does Facebook advertising still make sense?

Paid advertising on Facebook can be very cost-effective IF DONE RIGHT. To succeed with Facebook ads, you have to understand how it works and how it differs from other kinds of online advertising.

People don't go on Facebook actively looking for homes or information about mortgages like they do on Google and real estate portals. They're there to see pictures of their best friend's trip to Europe, connect with friends and (political rants aside) be social.

> People are on Facebook to passively consume information that's put in front of them. Facebook is curiosity driven. People browse and then something piques their interest.

Facebook Ads are often called passive or interest-based ads. This means that Facebook ads need to pique a passive user's interest.

You can't get away with focusing on solely on sales—it simply won't get most people's attention.

Your job is to get your content in front of the right audience and stop them in their tracks. You want your ads to be absolutely 'thumb-stopping!'

FIVE KEYS TO GETTING RESULTS WITH FACEBOOK ADS:

1. Create defined audiences

2. Use compelling content and creative

3. Bidding correctly

4. Automatic placements

5. Conversion and follow-up process

If you're new to Facebook advertising, it's required that you have a Facebook business page. So assuming you've got that, let's take a closer look at each of the five keys to getting results with Facebook ads.

FACEBOOK DEFINED AUDIENCES

To SUCCEED WITH Facebook ads, you want to think more about building audiences vs targeting. Your audience is made of people. Real people. They're not just a pool of numbers or demographics.

Creating audiences on Facebook can also help you reach people earlier in the buyer journey and win the customer early. Facebook audiences can also help you connect with your past clients and keep them engaged with your brand by promoting meaningful content. Let's take a closer look.

There are two general approaches you can take to creating audiences:

1. AUDIENCE BASED ON INTERESTS

2. CUSTOM AUDIENCES

Each of these audiences hits people in different stages of the buying or selling process and can be combined when appropriate. Let's take a look at each audience type and how it can help you improve your Facebook ad results.

Audience Based on Interests:

Facebook monitors the behavior of every user on their platform, cultivating a profile of peoples interests based by looking at certain interests, activities, the Pages they have liked and closely related topics.

For example: You can select people who have People who have expressed an interest in or like pages related to: House Hunting, Zillow, Trulia, Realtor.com, Homes.com, Pre-qualification (lending), Mortgage calculator, First-time homebuyer Grant and others. Thank you Facebook!

Interest-based targeting is generally used for cold audiences—when you want to introduce yourself to people who haven't heard of you before. The beauty of targeting people based on their interests and behaviors is that it's the best way to build audiences of people who don't already know you, but *may* have an interest buying or selling a home or getting pre-qualified for a mortgage.

So, one example of an audience you could build would be people who have expressed themselves to have an interest in House Hunting, Mortgage Calculator, and Zillow.

Based on those interests, it's more likely those people are in the early stages of home shopping and seeking information. Showing them an ad offering a "free list of homes under x price" would make sense.

Put a little money behind your "five steps to buying your first home" educational video(s). Video is some of the highest engaging content on Facebook!

Open houses, community events, market updates and client reviews are also great ads to attract this audience and supercharge your marketing!

The goal at this stage is not to sell. It's to build your brand awareness and get people engaging with your content. Once you get that, you can then move your cold audiences to the next stage which is Custom Audiences.

Facebook Custom Audiences

Facebook Custom Audiences are one of—if not *the* most—*essential* tools for successful Facebook advertising campaigns. There are several kinds of Custom Audiences for which you can place ads to reach this specific audience. Here are the three most important Custom Audiences for your business.

1. CUSTOMER/LEAD LIST CUSTOM AUDIENCE: Let's say you have been a busy real estate agent or lender for the last 10 years, but you haven't done a great job of staying in contact with your past clients or leads. You can upload your past client database or list of opt-in leads and Facebook will match your list with it's users.

- Putting your content in front of them on Facebook is one way to reintroduce yourself and remind them that you are their trusted real estate and mortgage resource.

When uploading a Customer File to Facebook to create a Custom Audience, this must be an opt-in list. This can *not* be a list of name, emails, and phone numbers you purchased.

1. **WEBSITE VISITORS CUSTOM AUDIENCE: (RE-TARGETING)** Are you driving traffic to your website? Even if someone has gone to your website, it's a safe bet that they didn't bookmark it. You can insert a Facebook Pixel tracking code on your website and re-target your Facebook advertising to all users that have visited a specific page on your website during a set time period (up to 180 days)!

- The first requirement to succeed with this strategy is you MUST DRIVE TRAFFIC to your website. Simply having a website is not enough. You have to have visitors to your website in order for this to be effective. If you ever needed a reason to push traffic to your site, this is IT! The goal here is to RE-ENGAGE THE PEOPLE WHO VISITED YOUR WEBSITE BUT HAVEN'T TAKEN THE ACTION YOU WANT THEM TO TAKE such as opting in for your list of homes, downloading a free report or scheduling a call. You can then re-target these audiences with highly relevant ad campaigns to move them forward.

1. **FACEBOOK ENGAGEMENT CUSTOM AUDIENCE: (RE-TARGETING)** Do you have content on your Facebook business page? You should. You can create custom audiences of people who engage with your posts, videos and events (think open house and community events) on Facebook and Instagram. For example, you can choose people who've watched 25% of your "new listing" video or "first time homebuyer

tips" video with other relevant content or a call to action.

- If someone has interacted with your content on Facebook, this is a great opportunity to re-target them with other relevant content to keep them engaged before they are ready to make it over to your site or move them along the buyer/seller journey towards a personal contact.

Compelling Content and Creative

Travis Thom is founder of Elevated REM, a Facebook Marketing Agency specializing in the real estate industry. His agency has generated over 350,000 Facebook and Instagram real estate leads and has cracked the code on what messaging and creative works for Facebook leads in real estate.

He has seen the best results for his clients when the ad content is relevant to each stage of the buyer journey, known as TOFU, MOFU, BOFU.

Sounds like something you might order off a health food menu doesn't it?

In fact they represent the different stages of the buyer's journey or as they say in marketing "the funnel." Each stage requires the right content and messaging to be delivered at the right time to increase your response rates and move the prospect along in their journey.

TOFU: TOP OF FUNNEL
Your goal with TOFU ads should be to educate your audience on a specific question, need or pain point that they often have. The most common form of TOFU content would be educa-

tional videos, links to articles, list of homes, your blog content, property videos and downloadable buyer/seller guides.

MOFU: MIDDLE OF FUNNEL

In this stage of the funnel, your content should continue to educate using testimonials, how-to information, downloadable guides, just listed and sold property ads.

BOFU: BOTTOM OF FUNNEL

At this point your audience, knows you and should be comfortable engaging one-on-one. This is where you go for a call-to-action in your ad like a phone consultation, in person meeting, invite to an event, drive to open houses, etc.

Chris Smith is the co-founder of Curaytor; an industry leading real estate online marketing platform and author of the best selling book *The Conversion Code*.

After millions of client and firm dollars spent on Facebook ads and analyzing the results, they have discovered a winning formula for content and creative. "The devil's in the details," says Chris.

Those details include:

- Using more than one photo in ads
- Placing the target link high up in ad copy
- Creating curiosity and engagement by leaving the address and price out of ad copy (if a listing-related post)
- Crafting an informative, enticing description
- Linking to a landing page that aligns with the ad and features a clear, bold call to action

For listing ads, you should provide enough detail, information, and value to drive engagement—rich description, number of beds and baths, amenities and photos—but compel consumers to visit their site to opt-in for more information.

Sometimes what's left out of the copy is more important than what's in, Smith said. When posting a new listing, for example, use multiple high-quality images of the property and an enticing description, but leave out the address and price, he added.

Bidding Correctly

If you want to succeed with Facebook ads, it's not just the shiny ad design and powerful copywriting that you need to master. You also need to know how to target the right Facebook audience and optimize your ad bidding.

The way Facebook ads work is that you're in an online auction bidding for the chance for your audience to click (or do whatever your goal is) on your ad. You only pay when somebody completes your event—clicks on your ad, watched your video, for instance—and your competition is other ads that also target the same audience.

While Facebook will try to satisfy every advertiser, the space for advertisement is limited even with over 2 BILLION monthly users. Sometimes, Facebook won't be able to fulfill all the requests. When this happens, THE HIGHEST BIDDERS WILL GET THE MOST PLACEMENTS.

There are two important takeaways here:

- If you try to bid too low, your campaign may not get the exposure it deserves, and you won't reach your goals. Remember, you always get what you pay for.

- Don't worry about bidding a high amount. You'll still

end up paying the lowest amount possible in the auction to get your ads delivered.

Facebook will only make you pay the lowest amount possible to win the bid and have your ad displayed. That means that if your competition bids $.45 and you bid $.50, you'll only have to pay $.46 because it's a penny higher than your competition. Make sense?

Before you decide on the right objective for your ad, you'll want to familiarize yourself with bidding and budget:

- A BID is how much you're willing to pay for a specific action. Different types of bids include cost per click or cost per 1000 impressions (CPM).

- Your BUDGET is the maximum amount you're willing to spend on your ad over a period of time

When you choose your budget, Facebook helps you spend up to your budget (never beyond) and ensures that your ad campaign delivers evenly throughout the day.

There are two types of budgets you can set:

- DAILY BUDGET: The amount you've indicated you're willing to spend on a specific ad set on a daily basis.

- LIFETIME BUDGET: You can also set a lifetime budget for your ad set. Your ads will be deployed evenly throughout the duration of your ad campaign.

Remember, even if people don't click your ad, the fact that they've seen your ad can help increase awareness of your personal brand, grow your audience and keep you top of mind until they're ready for contact.

- CAMPAIGN BUDGET OPTIMIZATION helps you improve ROI by automatically distributing your ad spend to your top performing ads in real time. This means your money goes directly where it should to the ads that are giving you results.

Here's a list of campaign objectives and their matching bidding options:

- Conversions: You bid on Conversions, Link Clicks, and Impressions
- Traffic: You bid on Link Clicks (CPC) and Impressions
- Video Views: You choose Video View Duration and Impressions

Automatic Placements

Travis Thom and his team recommend Automatic Placements because it allows Facebook to make the most of your budget. It places your ads on all the placements available on Facebook, Instagram, Audience Network and Messenger.

When you choose automatic placement, you tell Facebook to find the most relevant people across all of the eligible placements at the cheapest overall average cost available.

Automatic placements can help in getting the lowest CPC, reaching your audience at times of less competition, and combine the right placement with the right target audience.

Facebook uses advanced algorithms to determine which placement type performs the best and is the most effective for your brand and accordingly attempts to serve more ads in those winning bids. There is never one strategy or ad placement that fits every business or every market. What works for one market is not necessarily the same for other markets

No two ad accounts perform the same, what works for one might not necessarily work for the other. Succeeding with Facebook ads requires you to test, test and test.

Conversion and Follow-Up Process

Andrew Pawlak is the CEO of LeadPops, Inc. His company focuses on "creating digital experiences and lead conversion tools that entice potential customers to take action." Andrew affirms that where most people fail with paid online leads is by overlooking the importance of "conversion rate optimization."

Loan Originator Anthony Whitten with Movement Mortgage in Oregon, decided to get serious about generating his own leads with Facebook ads and engaged LeadPops to assist him with optimizing his conversion rate.

Over a five-month period, Anthony invested $2,000 in Facebook ads and generated five closed loans worth $26,000 in commissions. His Return on Ad Spend (ROAS) is over 928%!

Anthony is now teaching Getting Started with Facebook Ads classes to his local agents and partnering with agents to create a reciprocal partnership, generating leads together.

A strong follow-up sequence via phone, email, and text is a CRITICAL piece of the conversion process. Drip emails and text messages are ideally scheduled on an automated sequence, usually spaced out over days, weeks, and months, that begin to send once the lead has provided you their contact information.

To get the most out of Facebook marketing, you need to sync your leads directly to your CRM. You need to have a well-defined, repeatable sales process which is executed consistently for every new prospect.

The agents and lenders getting the best results on Facebook or Instagram ads all have integrated marketing automation, phone calls and text messaging built into their follow up process.

SPEED TO LEAD

TODAY'S BUYERS' AND sellers' expectations have evolved to expect a timely response. Speed to lead is critical to converting online real estate leads to closings. Your ROI is dependent on how quickly you follow-up with these initial lead inquiries and the systems you have in place to follow-up long term.

Following up on leads within the first five minutes or less will increase your lead conversion by up to 391%!

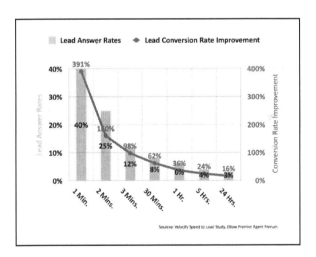

The only way this level of speed to lead is possible 100% of the time is by having automated systems in place to help you respond to leads.

Most CRM's will allow you to create a structured follow up process. Don't rely solely on automated email and text messaging.

Reach out with a personalized phone call, do whatever you can to
BUILD RAPPORT AND TRUST.

During the first 10 days, you should follow up everyday on leads
with a mix of phone calls, texts and emails. You can also send
video messages through text or email using a service like Bomb-
Bomb to increase your engagement and response rates.

Here's an example:

	Call	Email	Text		Call	Email	Text
Day 1	X	X		Day 6		X	
Day 2		X	X	Day 7		X	
Day 3			X	Day 8			X
Day 4		X		Day 9		X	
Day 5	X		X	Day 10	X		X

After ten days of consistent follow-up, if the lead is unresponsive,
you can place them on a long term nurture campaign in your
CRM.

For top real estate agents and lenders who generate a significant
amount of inbound leads, lead conversion companies like Verse.io
(formerly Agentology) or CallAction.io can be an extension of
your team. They can integrate outbound calls to your lead follow
up process, reach leads within seconds, 24/7, and only connect
you to motivated buyers and sellers who are ready to talk.

To succeed with Facebook ads, you need to the right plan and
process. Apply the best practices from this chapter and you will
significantly increase your lead conversion rates over the months-
long (and sometimes years-long) journey from lead to client.

Successful lead generation today requires you to establish your
expertise, engage your audience and open an always-on communication channel from the first point of interest in buying or selling to a closed transaction.

Want more help with Facebook ads?

Get the Ultimate Guide to Facebook Ads for Real Estate and free bonus videos to help guide you even further along your journey. To get free access to the *Companion Course*, go to: DISRUP-TORDIEBOOK.COM/COURSE

CHAPTER 9:
ONLINE REVIEWS

I F YOU THINK online reviews get lost in all the Internet noise, think again. Research from BrightLocal shows that 91% of people regularly or occasionally read online reviews, and 78% trust online reviews as much as a personal recommendation.

Younger sellers are more likely to place high importance on online reviews of an agent or lender with 61% of millennials and 51% of GenXers finding online reviews extremely or very important versus 41% of boomers.

Today, more than ever, customers depend on reviews before making a purchase or employing the services of a company with 68 percent of people forming an opinion after reading between one and six online reviews.

It's fair to say that online reviews are another version of word-of-mouth advertising. As a real estate agent or lender in today's world, reviews should be a top priority in your marketing plan.

Be proactive, and take control of your presence on review sites by following up with clients after a transaction. Ask them to fill out reviews on Google, Zillow, Realtor.com or any other review site that's relevant to you.

WHAT TYPE OF REVIEWS DO CONSUMERS LIKE TO SEE?

WHEN READING REAL estate related reviews, buyers and sellers look for anecdotes they can relate to. A review like, "Alan was great," doesn't hold much weight or provide enough useful information.

Potential clients don't just want to know that you are great; they want to know *why* you're great.

A better, more detailed review might read, "Alan was the best agent a busy parent could ever hope for. He he understood our needs of finding a home for our growing family in the exact area we wanted to live."

Not every client will respond to your request for an online review, of course, and that's okay. The best way to improve your response rate is to provide a world class customer experience.

Generally speaking, people tend to give reviews either when they are delighted or when they are upset; the middle ground, so to speak, tends to remain fairly silent. Being average won't get people excited about leaving you a review.

HOW TO ASK FOR REVIEWS UPFRONT

SET THE STAGE with your clients by being upfront with clients that you're going to want a review. A nice segue to the heads-up is to ask if they've read reviews before finding you.

Here's two sample scripts you can say:

"Most consumers read reviews to help them choose a real estate agent or lender. At the end of our process, I'd like to ask you the favor of writing a review so you can 'pay it forward' and help someone else who is considering using me as their agent/lender. Would that be ok with you?"

"If you read any of my past client reviews, thank you! I value all the feedback I can get, and I'm going to do everything I can to earn your five-star review as well."

HOW TO ASK FOR REVIEWS STILL PENDING

IN CASE YOU missed an opportunity to ask for a review in the moment or didn't get a client to write a review upon your first ask, here's a script for asking for a review later in the life cycle.

"[Name], thank you again for choosing me as your real estate agent/lender! I hope it was an easy move and that things have settled down a bit by now. May I ask you the favor of writing a review about your experience in working with me? It only takes a moment, and it helps ensure that future clients can trust us with their real estate needs. Thank you, [Name]. I appreciate you taking the time to give me feedback, and I look forward to reading your review."

HERE'S HOW TO GET THE MOST MILEAGE OUT OF YOUR CLIENT REVIEWS: Make a friendly follow-up call, check in on how much they love their new home. Ask if they're interested in doing a written or video review for you.

- *Ask them to give details.* Were they first-time home buyers? Are they locals or from out of town? What kind of support and response did the receive?

- *Send a follow-up* email or text with a link to the sites you wish them to fill out. Don't overwhelm them with links to all the sites that exist. Choose one or two.

- Make a friendly follow-up call, check how much they love their new home. Ask for a review and follow-up with your email or text link.

- *Give them an incentive* to fill out the review by including a gift certificate or a chance to win a bigger prize in the monthly review raffle. Every month one winner who's left a review will be entered into a giveaway.

Just getting started on your testimonial can be overwhelming for your clients. Sending a few leading questions can help them begin.

Here are some questions that you can answer as part of your request:

- What made you decide to [buy/sell] your home?

- Why did you choose me as your real estate agent/lender?

- What did you like best about your experience with me?

- What do you think I could have done better?

- Would you recommend me to your friends and family?

HIGHLIGHTING HERO MOMENTS

You should always keep a record of hero moments—when you demonstrated your expertise or professionalism. These are at points during a transaction when you negotiated like a boss, saved them money—responded lightning quick to win or save the deal.

They're a great prompt to include with your request for an online review. Asking clients to reflect on successful moments throughout their home-buying or selling process reminds them why *you* were the best choice for them.

WHERE TO SHARE YOUR REVIEWS

Once a review is published, share it on social media. Facebook, Instagram, LinkedIn and Twitter are ideal places to post testimonials.

Upload reviews to your website and create a rotating gallery of reviews to catch the eye of prospective clients.

Embed video testimonials: Upload video reviews to YouTube or Vimeo, embed them on your site and incorporate them in your email signature.

RESPONDING TO REVIEWS

THERE SEEMS TO be a common mantra out there that says, "You should reply to all negative reviews." The truth is...

YOU SHOULD REPLY TO *ALL* REVIEWS—GOOD, BAD OR NEUTRAL.

The most successful agents and lenders respond to their reviews publicly. As a consumer, seeing a personal thank-you note in response to their review means a lot. It conveys a personal touch—that you took the time to acknowledge and thank your client. Responding to reviews also shows that you are accessible and responsive online.

You do not need to over-think and deeply analyze your review replies. Just reply with a thank you, and if the opportunity presents itself to naturally work in a mention of something you do as part of your business operations, all the better (but don't force it).

Your review response can be as simple as, *"Thanks so much for writing that glowing review. I loved working with you, too."*

WHY NEGATIVE REVIEWS AREN'T ALL THAT BAD

SOMETIMES, A BALL gets dropped during a transaction, and deals can go sour. If you face the issue of a less-than-favorable review on your profile, relax. It's not the end of the world. Consumers are smart. They recognize that nobody is perfect.

Many buyers and sellers actually lend more credibility to reviews when they see a negative one mixed in—it shows that they are real.

The best approach with handling unhappy client reviews is taking the high road and responding publicly to explain what went wrong. Avoid getting defensive—try to stay neutral and apologetic. Sometimes your response to an unhappy client can say more about you as an agent than the review itself.

HERE ARE SOME SAMPLE RESPONSES TO NEGATIVE REVIEWS:

UNRETURNED CONTACT: *"I'm sorry we couldn't connect. My goal is to return contacts as quickly as possible, and you're welcome to text me or call and we'll try to get this worked out. Thanks!"*

ANONYMOUS: *"I understand why sometimes people don't want to use a real name when leaving an online review. If this reviewer would like to contact me directly, I'd appreciate that so we can resolve their concern. Thank you!"*

FRUSTRATED CLIENT: *"I am sorry you did not experience a completely flawless transaction, that is always our goal and we work hard to ensure every client is treated to world-class customer service. I appreciate the feedback and we plan to incorporate some of the things we learned in this transaction to improve the experience for all our clients."*

THERE ARE SEVERAL REASONS YOU SHOULD CONSIDER REPLYING TO *ALL* REVIEWS.

- It's an opportunity to say "thank you." Your client took the time to create an account and write a review. Isn't it simple courtesy to thank them for their effort?

- Other people will see you thanking your clients. People like to work with people they trust, respect and like, and saying "thank you" is a likable trait. It's OK to demonstrate that you are a nice person.

- It is another opportunity to broadcast information and get it on the Internet. This isn't to say that you should use review replies to fill the page with talk all about you, but an opportunity to softly drive home a point should never be overlooked.

- Replying to a review adds another dimension of being human in what can sometimes be seen as impersonal words on a page. Adding a reply helps personalize the review and lends credibility to it.

In a competitive industry like real estate, professionals need client reviews to stand out from their peers, build credibility and get chosen.

TOP RATED REVIEW SITES

FOR THE MOST effective use of testimonials, the best return on investment (ROI) will be directing your clients to leave a review on sites that are a significant lead source for you and/or places people frequent to look to at reviews.

Zillow Reviews

As the largest real estate marketplace on the internet, Zillow tops the list of places your future clients are searching for homes. If you want more exposure and use the Zillow Premier Agent program, having great reviews on Zillow is even more important.

Realtor.com

Although they get only about one-third of the traffic of Zillow, Realtor.com is the second-largest online real estate platform and worthy of you having a profile and presence with reviews.

Google Reviews

Reviews on Google are an important factor when customers are using Google to search for a lender or real estate agent. Anyone with a Gmail account, can leave a review for a local business on Google.

One of the best ways to simplify the process is to create a link that will send people directly to the review form on Google to rate your business. Google calls its local search features for local business—Google My Business. This is where your reviews will show up when people Google you or relevant search terms and keywords you rank for.

If you're new to Google My Business and want to learn how to increase your visibility and potentially get leads from Google users, we'll cover this in more detail in Chapter 10: Winning the Customer Early.

Yelp

Although Yelp has been somewhat eclipsed as a place to review real estate agents and lenders in the past few years by Google and Zillow, a Yelp review will still come up high in search results for your name or company name. Consider having positive reviews there to leave a consistently favorable impression in the search results.

TIP: Yelp is very finicky about its reviews. If someone creates an account for the sole purpose of writing a review for you, that review will likely never be activated. Yelp likes reviews from active Yelp users. I recommend you ask your clients (and past clients), "Are you a Yelp user?" If the answer is "yes," then ask them to write a review for you.

SO HERE'S A GOAL FOR YOU: set aside 20 minutes every month to send out a few review requests and revisit requests with clients who haven't followed through yet. Use this time as an opportunity to reconnect with past clients and improve your expertise at getting reviews.

Ask for reviews no more than three times from each client: It's professional to ask once and follow up two times at most when requesting a testimonial.

AUTOMATING YOUR REVIEWS

IF YOU WANT to win the reputation game, you need to be asking for more online reviews.

One of the most important steps you can take as you are trying to manage the online reputation of your personal brand is to reach every customer you possibly can while improving the process that they must go through in order to leave their feedback.

Both asking directly and automating with Online Reputation Management (ORM) companies increases client reviews. ORM companies help you assess, build, and monitor your online reputation. In some cases, they will also help you repair your online reputation if needed. ORM providers use intelligent software to send your clients real-time SMS and email review requests at critical moments during the transaction.

Clients are directed to the review sites that matter most to you, where they can share feedback. You can monitor and respond to all reviews and auto-share reviews to your website, search engines, social channels and more.

Companies like Social Survey, BirdEye, Podium, MeetRex, TrustPilot and Reputation.com are top contenders if you're considering the services of an ORM to help you build your online reviews.

Reviews are one of the most important things you can get to disrupt proof your business and build your online reputation. By focusing on the right review websites, doing a great job for your clients and using best practices, continually building your reviews is an investment that will pay off for many years. Online reviews can also help you win the customer early, which, we'll cover in the next chapter.

CHAPTER 10:
WINNING THE CUSTOMER EARLY

I F YOU TRULY want to disrupt proof your business and win the customer early, don't overlook the most important people for the future of your business.

They are found in your CRM and Sphere of Influence. They are your past clients and the people who will enthusiastically refer you to friends, family, and colleagues who are looking for a great agent or lender.

For those who already have a robust database, you have an advantage over the disruptors IF you are proactively engaged with relevant content, nurturing your personal connections and DELIVERING THE MOST VALUE TO THE CUSTOMER which includes providing a streamlined, sales and customer experience.

DIGITAL MEDIA AND A ROBUST ONLINE PRESENCE ARE THE FUTURE OF GENERATING REPEAT AND NEW CLIENTS IN REAL ESTATE AND LENDING.

Here are three important questions to ask yourself:

1. Where is my audience?

2. Where is my audience active?

3. Where is my audience searching for relevant content?

To get the attention of your next client (and your past clients) you have to engage where they're actively searching and consuming content. Like it or not, social media is a huge part of where people's attention is right now.

> A strong online presence—so clients can find you—with relevant content—linked with an effective lead engagement and nurturing process—and client testimonials are essential to winning the attention of your future clients.

Are You a Conversational Brand?'

Nobody *has* to be on social media. For many, social media is where they do to be entertained, to fill some down time and passively browse around. Unless of course your searching for a specific thing such as on YouTube.

To get and keep people's attention on social media, you have to *make yourself conversational.* This doesn't have to be expensive or difficult, but you do have to stand out in some unique way.

I've heard the arguments that "others are already doing video in my area" or "I don't know what to post" and other excuses. You have a unique voice, an opinion, a personality and that is your first point of being unique. You will attract and connect with a different audience than another person.

It really comes down to two things that matter.

1. Are people talking about or engaging with you? ("you" can be a person, your personal brand, your results you deliver for clients, etc.)

2. Are those conversations and engagements leading to your desired outcome? (consuming your content,

website visitors, inquiries, appointments, contracts and loan applications; or whatever your desired outcome is.)

While the initial process of buying or selling a home may start online, the good news is; most people still seek the advice of a trusted real estate agent and lender.

HOW TO WIN THE CUSTOMER EARLY

TODAY'S MODERN AGENTS and lenders are winning by creating personal brands with hyper local or specific content, building their online reputation and earning the trust of people who refer them or choose them and become clients.

Scott Schang, Co-Owner of BuyWise Mortgage Brokerage in Orange County, CA has been writing consumer education articles since 2007 on his blog at www.FindMyWayHome.com.

Scott writes specific content, for a specific group of people with a specific set of problems.

Here's a few examples:

- Restoring Credit After Bankruptcy
- How to Buy a Home After Bankruptcy
- How to Buy a Home After Short Sale
- Qualifying for a Mortgage with IBR Student Loans
- New Student Loan Guidelines Make Homeownership Easier
- Qualifying for a Mortgage with Self-Employed Income

His consistency had paid off. His blog averages 10,000 site visitors every month. These people are finding Scott because they are searching for specific content for their specific situation and his content shows up in a Google search.

Scott creates lead capture funnels using LeadPops within his articles to build his database, schedule conversations, and ultimately take loan applications and close loans. Scott attributes approximately 38% of his total closed loan volume to traffic and leads directly from his blog content.

WINNING THE WAR FOR ATTENTION

THE NAME OF THE GAME IS WINNING CONSUMER ATTENTION IN A CONTEMPORARY WORLD.

You are where your attention is and, as it happens, our attention is nowhere and everywhere at once. Ads, smartphones, apps, social media, the internet —we're captive to an endless parade of distractions.

To win the customer early you have to show up where the customer is, engage and communicate via today's contemporary mediums.

What does that mean? It means understanding how and where people today search for and consume content to become educated and informed about things that matter to them.

In Chapter 9 we discussed the importance of online reviews and having a Google My Business profile as a key element to winning the customer early.

Chapter 8 looked at the six categories of lead generation to help you win the customer early.

Chapter 7 you read examples of agents and lenders wining with content marketing.

The battle for attention is the first battle in everything, and those who have mastered the techniques of getting attention by all relevant means have a massive advantage.

START A COMMUNITY FOCUSED PODCAST OR VIDEO SHOW

SAVVY REAL ESTATE agents and lenders should implement a community focused weekly show or podcast. Call it "The [Your Town] Small Business Show" or borrow from examples you read about in this book.

Nicole Nicolay and Robyn Annicchero are agents in Livermore CA and created the "Lunch With Livermore" video show. Every other Monday they feature chat about training for the Livermore Half-Marathon, favorite shoes, becoming Volleyball and Lacrosse moms, the Furry Convention and all their favorite local events and tips about living in Livermore.

You are not competing with the entire population of video shows or podcasts; YOU ARE ONLY AFTER *YOUR* LOCAL AUDIENCE. It's not about millions of listeners or viewers. It's about creating *engagement* with the small community of people who matter—and are interested.

Today we're seeing more brands merging online and offline experiences to give consumers the best of both worlds with an integrated hyperlocal engagement strategy.

PARTNER WITH LOCAL BUSINESSES

I RECOMMEND WORKING with local companies, offering some type of incentive. For example, do a 'how to prep your lawn for winter' with a local lawn service and then work with the company to offer your clients a discount, ie: 10% off first service when you mention ABC Realty.

This helps you become a referral source for your local business partners and adds value. Plus you promote it on social media and to your email database to increase awareness and engagement.

If you want to be the go-to agent for a neighborhood, the easiest way is to show that you're part of the community, and the best way to demonstrate that is through regular, targeted posting of relevant content. Here are some examples.

1. Building developments

People love to have the scoop about what's going into the vacant storefront down the street or what's happening with all the construction cranes they're seeing.

Do some legwork and find out. Include a photo of the current site/storefront and share it with the information you uncover.

2. Visit Neighborhood Businesses

Share seasonal posts at local favorites. Things like a drippy ice cream cone in your hand with the caption "Ted's ice cream parlor just started serving raspberry sorbet again!" or a whipped-cream-topped coffee with "OK, it's officially winter—I had my peppermint mocha at Java Hut!"

Visit a new restaurant, and post a brief video about menu highlights, ambiance, entertainment or grab an interview with the owner or head chef. Be sure and tag the restaurant in your Facebook post to grow your organic reach and engagement.

3. Support Local Youth Sports

Is the soccer or baseball team having a fundraising car wash? Post about it a day or two before, include images of the team from its website, a link to its website, and a geotag of where the car wash is being held.

Grab your smartphone and do a Facebook Live from the scene of the kids washing cars, and encourage people to drop by for a good cause and get a car wash.

The team will appreciate it, Facebook's algorithm prioritizes live video in the newsfeed, and parents will likely share your post!

4. School Fundraisers

Is the local elementary school having a walk-a-thon to raise money for new playground equipment? Pay to have your logo added to the T-shirts for the event, and then share photos or videos of neighborhood kids participating (always get parental approval first).

Include a caption such as "Happy to support the kids at Ben Franklin Elementary today for their walk-a-thon."

5. Showcase a Local Charity

Choose one a month, and post about their current fundraising efforts. It could be a homeless shelter looking for donations of blankets, a school book drive, or even a neighborhood garage sale donating their earnings to a charity.

6. Monthly Neighborhood Sales

Create a monthly post showing the sales prices of all the home that sold in your neighborhood the month before. Use a high-quality image that clearly represents your community (it could be the sign welcoming visitors to town or the community pool that everyone recognizes), and link back to a blog post (or another landing page) that shows the data.

Encourage people to follow you or subscribe to see the data updates every month.

Social Media Attention

Social media audiences are largely "weak links." What I mean by this is that a "like" or even a "follow" correlates to almost zero actual emotional connection to a brand or a business.

When somebody "likes" you on social media, it's like they're waving at you. By liking or following you, consumers are acknowledging you or saying "hello," but that doesn't mean they would immediately trust you with a transaction.

The social media audience of "weak links" is still important because it represents *potential*. These are contacts you never would have had any other way.

To activate that potential, you have to go far beyond awareness and "likes" to deliver unique and extraordinary human connection and value that builds trust, leading somebody to *choose* to do business with you. You have to build an *actionable audience*.

Success with Social Media

The social media accounts that win by driving relationships beyond weak links into an actionable audience have two things in common:

1. A consistent human element

2. Unique value, insight, access, or entertainment

There are of course exceptions from long standing brands and years of advertising like Disney or Coca-Cola.

But for most small businesses competing in the war for attention, you need those two human components – human and unique value, insight, access or entertainment.

So just posting pics of you in front of your new listing or awesome sushi lunch, that doesn't cut it. All the great small business social media accounts feature real human beings.

My friend Chelsea Peitz is an example of a both elements for social media success on her primary platform of choice; Instagram.

Chelsea shares real estate marketing tips with a consistent human element featuring herself and her adorable young son. She's real and authentic, sharing Instagram stories and social media tips sometimes while applying her makeup, providing her followers with unique value and exclusive access into her daily life – and being entertaining.

She's become an in-demand real estate industry speaker and author of *What to Post. How to Create Engaging Social Media Content That Builds Your Brand and Gets Results* (available on Amazon). You can follow Chelsea @chelsea.peitz

The "value" that you share through your human presence can take several forms:

KNOWLEDGE — Share your observations and knowledge about a relevant topic for your audience.

ACCESS — Give your audience a peek into a "day in the life" documenting your day, your training for the 5K race or take us inside the kitchen of a local restaurant.

INSIGHT — Show us all the steps involved in funding a loan, selling a listing, getting your buyer offer accepted or raising money for your favorite charity.

ENTERTAINMENT — Don't take yourself too seriously. Share blooper reels of your early attempts at video, be self-deprecating when appropriate, share humorous stories or content.

Lastly, consistency is the secret sauce that many people miss. It may take several months (or longer) to build real momentum and find your voice. Can you stick with it long enough to win?

To attract your audience, begin by giving them something easy to digest. We've shared multiple examples in this book to help you create content that educates your audience using today's media.

The goal is to have your content be interesting enough that people begin to share, comment and follow you. As your reputation and presence grows, so does your position in the battle for attention and winning the customer early.

For your business to stand out, be customer-centric. Define *what* you do, *who* you do it for, and *how* you do it. Give your customers depth of information. Provide value. Be consistent. Experiment. Invest in technology, marketing, and people to help you scale and grow.

CHAPTER 11

REDUCE THE FRICTION

P UT YOURSELF IN the shoes of a potential client. You've just found a mobile video listing for the property that could be your dream home, and you want to see it in person as soon as possible, but the agent's office is closed until 9 AM the next day.

What do you do?

Leave a voicemail, hoping they'll call you back first thing in the morning? Send an email, and hope that the agent has email notifications turned on? Fill out a form, even though you know from past experience that it sometimes takes days to get a reply?

Or do you pass on all three, and make a mental note to check back the next day? Of course, by that time, you may have moved on to a different listing with a different agent. If the agent had an app that enabled web-based messaging, things would be a lot easier.

REDUCE THE FRICTION

A RECENT OWNERS.COM survey found that 33% of homebuyers wish their agent had leveraged technology to better streamline the process.[1]

According to a study from Drive Research, when 1,000 home purchase customers were asked what words best describe the home-buying process, the top selections were "time consuming"

---

1. http://bit.ly/31JU5EO

(25.4%) and "challenging" (24.1%). Understanding fees (34.1%) and finding the right loan (30.9%) were among the top pain points.[2]

Gregg Pechmann is a Mortgage Planner and Branch Manager with Hancock Mortgage. His approach to mortgage planning is to "make the mortgage process as easy as possible and to call his clients lifetime friends."

As a long-time user of Barry Habib's MBS Highway, Gregg uses the Loan Comparison tool to show his prospective clients the impact of each mortgage option over time, helping them make an informed decision and choose the best mortgage for their situation.

When asked whether their real estate agent and loan consultant communicated with each other, 24.6% of respondents said no (31.8% of non-first-time homebuyers vs. 17.7% of first-time homebuyers).

OPTIMIZING THE CUSTOMER EXPERIENCE

THE PERCEPTION THAT communication is not happening between agent and loan officer creates stress and frustration during the home-buying process. This is your opportunity to differentiate yourself by ensuring your process has transparency and thorough communication from all parties to the consumer. Here's a few suggestions for optimizing the customer experience.

Provide an Upfront Checklist

Customers are looking for you to be their guide. Providing them with an initial checklist of the steps during a transaction and doc-

---

2. https://prn.to/39rmBxo

uments they will need to provide is your first chance to set proper expectations. Helping them feel comfortable, reassured, and safe is a vital component to delivering a world-class experience.

Provide Status Updates

On every loan, the loan originator should make it their goal to have zero calls from the borrower or agents requesting a status update. Having automated systems to proactively inform all stakeholders of status changes and next steps can help, although making a personal call, is consumers preferred method for status updates.

Set Proper Expectations

Roughly one in every six loans will experience a problem in the course of origination. Setting proper expectations with the borrower early in the process, letting them know that the loan process is complex and that experiencing a few bumps along the way is normal and can be expected, will help you reduce client frustration when issues occur.

THE RISE OF CHATBOTS

WE MENTIONED THE rise of Chatbots in Chapter 5 and included them again here because Chatbots are increasingly being used as part of marketers content marketing and client engagement strategy and to reduce friction during a transaction.

These days, people are on mobile, pulling up listings on-the-fly, checking prices and Googling you. People want information delivered to them on mobile in a way that is easy and INSTANT.

Chatbots leverage chat mediums like text, website chat windows and social messaging services across platforms like Facebook Messenger and Whatsapp to receive and respond to messages. Chatbots are programmed to answer basic questions, prequalify or segment the person chatting so that you can decide whether to pick up the chat and personally answer questions.

Hubspot reports that messaging apps get between an 80%-90% OPEN RATE AND 30% CLICK THROUGH RATE and for the first time, people are using them more than social networks.[3]

If you happen to have a robust Facebook presence with a good following and engagement, it makes sense to deploy a Facebook messenger chatbot. If you generate a good amount of traffic on your website, then a chatbot that pops up and assists your visitors on your website in their journey may be your best bet—or both!

FACEBOOK MESSENGER

OVER 1.2 BILLION people use Facebook messenger every month, chatting, sending pictures, videos, and building relationships, without needing a persons cell phone number. Currently, you cannot use your personal profile or Facebook Group for a Facebook messenger bot; another reason why having a Facebook business page is important.

When people use your chat bot, they will instantly be added as a connection to your business so now you will be able to send people messages as you would email.

You will be able to run targeted Facebook ads specifically to them and you'll retain the connection to the person (via their phone). You can even gain a new lead simply when they leave a comment on your Facebook page.

Are First-time homebuyers your target market?

Millennials are the quickest adaptors of chatbot-based customer

---

3. http://bit.ly/37gc5I3

experiences. According to Huffington Post, 60% OF THE MIL-LENNIAL POPULATION already uses chatbots and 71% OF MIL-LENNIALS have implied that they would like to try using one.[4]

Using a chatbot is a powerful way to make a quick connection with a contact, because it is immediate and feels easy and conversational. A chatbot will handle conversations with clients that are at the top of the funnel—generally people who are in the early stages of searching for property, seeking answers to questions and in the consideration phase of buying or selling a home.

Every chatbot interaction can be personalized, based on your user's preferences. A chatbot for your buyer campaign might ask when they need to move then give a range of "1–6 months", "6–12 months", or "just looking." You can program the bot to respond differently, depending on the answer your prospect submits and even show a welcome video from you that engages your prospect.

Chatbots can integrate into your MLS/IDX and send information about properties for sale, schedule property tours, and even promote open houses with a link to a map and directions.

There's more to a chatbot than just replying to FAQ's and reducing your workload. It can be used to provide visitors with property information, images, videos and virtual tours. Chatbots are more like assistants that work to interact and perform round-the-clock so that you don't miss out on leads and building relationships.

A chatbot is not here to replace you.

It is here to assist in providing relevant information to consumers who want quick answers, start a relevant 1:1 conversation that drives engagement and creates connection.

---

4. http://bit.ly/2HbBSXp

A decent place to start would be to gather together your most frequently asked questions—the ones with easily automated responses—and use that as a jumping-off point for your chatbot strategy.

In June 2018, Facebook commissioned a survey of 8,156 people. According to survey results, 65% of people surveyed feel more confident messaging a business than emailing. 55% of people surveyed prefer messaging over filling out a form on a website and 58% prefer messaging a business over calling.[5]

Homebuyers can use Messenger to ask questions, schedule viewings, search inventory, and much more. Messenger can help lenders and agents generate quality leads at scale, collect information from customers through automated question and answer prompts that allow you to instantly qualify and disqualify leads based on responses, and prioritize leads based on intent.

Messaging is growing, because it's the easiest way to get in touch. Messenger creates personalized connections at scale. Messenger makes it possible to start and nurture conversations across devices, wherever and whenever it's convenient, reducing the friction in communicating and getting a response.

CHATBOT PROVIDERS

FRESHCHAT IS ADVANCED chat software that you can easily plug into your website and lets you gives your site visitors exactly what they want; instant gratification! You can have it ping your phone whenever someone has a question, or better yet, easily program a chat bot to engage them until they're ready to talk to you.

STRUCTURELY is a lead cultivation chatbot, like many others, also plugs into MLS data. The platform manages leads and an

---

5. http://bit.ly/31IvJV

AI-powered chatbot called Aisa Holmes. When leads land on an agent's website or Facebook page, Aisa starts a conversation via web chat or Facebook Messenger. It also talks to a ton of your favorite lead gen/CRM platforms like Real Geeks, BoomTown, Kunversion, Placester, and more.

MOBILEMONKEY is a Facebook Messenger marketing platform that helps businesses with automated chat bots, conversion funnels, and content templates to get started easy.

MANYCHAT is another platform for Facebook Messenger marketing with a user friendly intuitive drag`n`drop builder, that enables you to set up your Facebook Messenger bot without any technical knowledge required.

Messenger marketing is still in its infancy which gives your first mover advantage in winning customer attention. It won't be long until the floodgates open, and marketers rush in to try and take their slice of the pie.

We are in a consumer-controlled buying economy, which means to win, we must adapt and embrace consumers growing expectations for relevance, speed, personalization and transparency in the home buying or selling process.

MOBILE FIRST

I DID SOME research, and created a list of the top things consumers are looking for on a mobile website. Most of the stats below are based on a Google study:

- LOCATION: 76 percent of mobile users want to get location information. Make sure you include your office address on your mobile site.

- CLICK-TO-CALL: In my opinion, this is probably the most important feature on a mobile site! Sixty-one percent of mobile users want to be able to call you with a simple click. CallAction.io is a provider of this functionality. If you don't offer click-to-call or a mobile app, you may be losing home shoppers to sites that do.

- EMAIL: 54 percent of mobile users want to be able to click to send you an email. Use the envelope icon for easy click-to-email.

- AN APP: 53 percent of mobile users want to be able to download a mobile app. If you're not offering a mobile app download on your site, you may lose mobile consumers to a site that does.

- SOCIAL LINKS: 48 percent of mobile users want to be able to access your social networks. Maybe they'd rather reach out to you on Facebook messenger vs. email. Or maybe they want to check you out online before they call. Give them the option by including button links to your social media profiles.

- VIDEO: 41 percent of mobile users want to be able to play a video. It's hard to read text on a mobile phone! Place a short video of *you* on your home page, and share with viewers why you love working in real estate. Studies show that video increases conversion rates by over five times, so it's a win-win!

- EASY TO NAVIGATE: 78 percent of mobile users want to be able to find what they are looking for in just one or two clicks. So really think about your site's navigation, and make sure your site's most popular sections are just a click away from the home page.

- SEARCH BAR THAT'S EASY TO FIND AND USE: If the mobile user cannot access the content he is looking for in one or two clicks, he will want to quickly search for the content by using a search bar. It's much easier to do a quick search in the search bar than it is to manually search a site. This is especially true on mobile devices.

- Nonscrolling forms with limited fields: If you build any lead generation into your website (and you should), you will want the associated forms to be nonscrolling and easy to fill out with a limited number of fields.

- An option to visit the non-mobile site: This does not apply if you build a mobile-responsive site, but is especially important for redirected mobile websites. Redirected mobile sites tend to have limited content, so giving the consumer the option to head over to the full site (even if it isn't designed for mobile use) is important.

Since the on-demand economy and mobile devices are accessible to consumers everywhere at every impulse to buy or sell, immediate communication will be more important than ever to win the customer early and disrupt proof your business.

CHAPTER 12:
HOW TO DISRUPT PROOF YOUR BUSINESS

To DISRUPT PROOF your business it's not about survival of fittest. It's whoever is most adaptable to change that survives—and thrives.

Your primary objective should be to OWN THE RELATIONSHIP with your audience. To own the relationship, you first need to get someone's attention. Whose attention do you have today? How will you keep that attention?

Do you spend your time being angry about the changes happening in our industry? Are you romantic about the past? Stuck in the pattern of "how things have always been done?"

That's a fixed mindset, unwilling to adapt to change.

A growth mindset is a willingness to adapt and take on the opportunity to grow and evolve. If you're committed to your business and above all, serving people, you'll adapt and learn how to stay relevant.

> "Because the purpose of a business is to create a customer, your business has two purposes. Marketing and innovation. Marketing and innovation produce results. Everything else is an expense. Marketing is the distinguishing, unique function of the business."
>
> —Peter Drucker

What about your business? Are you innovating in your marketing and customer experience? Or are you a "fading winner?"

Real estate coach Tom Ferry spoke of "fading winners" on a recent podcast. He identified a fading winner as the following:

> *"A fading winner is a ten + year, industry veteran who's exceptional with clients, but hasn't adapted his/her marketing and lead generation to match our modern world."*

You may still be winning because you've been around so long. If you're not keeping up with innovation, you're becoming irrelevant to the market, missing out on new clients, and losing attention from past clients—*fading away.*

Innovation isn't just about embracing technology at the expense of real, human connections.

BIG TECH IS LOSING TOUCH WITH THE AVERAGE CONSUMER

J.D. POWER RELEASED its 2019 U.S. Primary Mortgage Origination Satisfaction Survey, revealing that technology boosts satisfaction but consumers want personal interaction.

In fact, survey data reveals, that although the usage of digital channels increased, only 3% of consumers rely exclusively on digital self-service channels. Furthermore, satisfaction peaked when consumers spoke with lenders either in-person or on the phone as they applied for a mortgage.

J.D. Power Financial Services Practice Lead John Cabell said; "technology alone is not a magic bullet. The key is knowing where to leverage it and where to layer in more traditional forms on one-on-one support."

MY HOME LOAN EXPERIENCE

MY PERSONAL MORTGAGE shopping experience is an example of relying too much on technology and automation.

It was a Saturday and we needed to submit an offer on a home with a pre-approval quickly.

Being new to the area, we chose a local lender recommended by our agent.

After completing the online application—including submitting all related financial documents, we expected to receive a call back from the lender to review our situation and obtain a pre-approval the same day.

What happened next? Nothing.

After submitting the online application, we received an email notification that "someone will be in touch." Monday came, no call. Tuesday came and I finally got a call from someone at the company, apparently the Loan Officers assistant who requested a call to review the loan application.

When did I hear from the actual Loan Officer whose website with snappy headshot I submitted the loan application? On Wednesday, I received a canned video email congratulating me on the purchase of my home and outlining the next steps in processing our loan.

Epic fail. I had already moved on.

Despite consumers' dependency on technology in most aspects of their lives, two thirds feel companies are losing the human touch in customer service, according to a new PwC survey; *Experience is Everything*. And 75% said they want *more*, not less, human interaction.

Results from the PwC poll conclude that in the age of artificial intelligence (AI), chatbots, Internet of Things (IoT) and Big Data, companies need to do more to balance technology with customer service.

We love our smartphones, but we still want the human touch in our significant buying experiences. As for the "tug-of-war" between technology and the human touch, consumers want a balance of both.

Brian Case is the #1 ranked Loan Officer for units in the state of Oregon. In 2019 he closed over 300 loans for nearly $100 Million in fundings.

Nearly 95% of his loan applications are completed using his online app. Approximately 80% of those who complete the online application convert to an in-person mortgage consultation at Brian's office. That's giving the consumer what they want, a balance of both high tech and high touch.

To disrupt proof your business, you must become great at leveraging technology, systems, processes AND delivering the best client experience with a healthy dose of *the human touch*.

Brian Manning has ranked among the Top 1% of Mortgage Originators in the nation since 2015. For every client, Brian provides a mobile-first, video driven Total Cost Analysis using Mortgage Coach presentation software. He's delivering a high-tech and high-touch mortgage experience, educating his clients, accelerating trust and improving his conversions. He's delivering an experience that most consider "too much work" and he's reaping the rewards.

In an industry that relies so heavily on repeats and referrals, THE CUSTOMER EXPERIENCE SHOULD BE THE PRIMARY FOCUS.

You're in the business of marketing trust.

You don't sell homes or mortgages. That's just the end result of creating trust. Trust is a *feeling* created through a combination of personal engagement with a brand (you) and the shared *experience* of others with that brand (what others say).

Unlike the "old days," where trust was built with a handshake, today you can scale engagement and trust right from your smartphone. Alan Christian has been in mortgage lending since 2016. In only a year, Alan has sent out over 1,765 BombBomb videos. He creates personalized introduction videos, briefly explains what people can expect from him through the mortgage process which increases his conversion ratio, earning trust and growing his influence.

Today, you can record a video and post it online, reaching hundreds or thousands of people in minutes, creating engagement and trust—at scale. That's marketing and innovation in today's contemporary world.

Your clients can share their experience working with you on social media, post online reviews, helping scale your reach and trust even further. Today, your customers are your best marketing.

> As the market shifts, consumers will value role of agent and lender as trusted advisor more than ever before.

The digital real estate shift is a battle of David (you) vs. Goliaths (the disruptors). You won't win by trying to outspend Goliath or being a self-proclaimed "great real estate agent or lender."

YOU WIN WITH MARKETING AND INNOVATION.

Are iBuyers entering your market, capturing attention, and taking market share? How do you adapt, innovate, and win?

The Kenny Klaus Team of Phoenix, AZ has been ranked in the Top Real Estate Teams in the US every year by transactions by Real Trends and the Wall Street Journal, closing over $100m in volume every year since 2016.

The Phoenix market is ground zero for iBuyers such as Opendoor, Offerpad and Zillow.

Kenny's not bad-mouthing iBuyers. He's not having a tantrum. He launched OfferDepot.com to help his clients evaluate and understand the iBuyer offers vs a traditional sale, allowing his clients to choose the best option for them.

In 2019, 32% of Kenny's transactions had an iBuyer as either the buyer or seller.

Kenny Klaus decided to innovate his business by including iBuyer offers in his marketing strategy. He's being a trusted advisor, allowing people to make an informed decision for themselves. Kenny is winning the attention and trust of people through marketing and innovation.

Every industry is impacted by disruption. Technology and innovation are emotionless. They don't care about your opinions of social media or how things used to be.

The shift has happened and it continues to evolve. How you RESPOND is the single biggest indicator of how well you survive and thrive the shift.

Here's a review of the six key ways to survive and thrive the digital real estate shift.

6 Steps to Disrupt Proof Your Business

1. Develop Your Personal Brand (The Foundation)

2. Become Known

3. Generate Consistent Deal Flow (Database, Referrals and Leads)

4. Build Your Online Reputation (Online Reviews)

5. Win the Customer Early (Content, Engage and Nurture)

6. Reduce the Friction (World Class Customer Experience)

The speed of change makes the future uncertain. But one thing is certain. Consumers will will be in control, have choices and ultimately win, as they always have.

BE MORE HUMAN

DR. ROBERT CIALDINI IS the Regents' Professor Emeritus of Psychology and Marketing at Arizona State University and was a visiting professor of marketing, business and psychology at Stanford University.

His books, including *Influence* and *Pre-Suasion,* have sold more than five-million copies in 41 different languages and *Fortune* lists his books in their "75 Smartest Business Books."

In a recent interview, Dr. Cialdini was asked "in this very noisy, overwhelming world, what can anybody do to stand out?"

Without hesitation, he said just three words: "Be. More. Human."

In a world of algorithms, machine learning and automation, being more human creates emotion, gives meaning and impact.

Today, we have the ability to connect with people like never before. If we make human connection and meaningful engagement our primary focus, we'll be okay.

Remember that everybody starts at the bottom. Don't be afraid to start small and learn, improve, learn improve, and keep going. Be consistent and be patient. Serve your audience with your arms wide open, versus your hand extended, expecting something in return.

This is the end of *Disrupt or Die* the book, but this is just beginning. If you enjoyed this book, I would be eternally grateful if you took a minute to write a review on Amazon.

If you want more resources to help you survive and thrive the digital real estate shift, I've created a free *Disrupt or Die Companion Course* with checklists, bonus videos and resources to help guide you even further along your journey. To get free access to the *Companion Course*, go to:

DISRUPTORDIEBOOK.COM/COURSE

Thank you for spending time with me and my book. I hope you

received value and that you'll implement some of the ideas that inspired you. Let's keep in touch, ok?

TOOLS AND
RESOURCES

I NCLUDED HERE FOR your reference is a partial list of tools and resources used by agents and lenders to implement some of the strategies and tactics discussed in this book. You can find more resources in the free, *Companion Course* at DisruptorDieBook.com/Course

BUSINESS TOOLS

MBS HIGHWAY Is a communication tool that will help you improve your batting average and turn more conversations into mortgage applications and increased fundings. www.mbshighway.com

MORTGAGE COACH Is the proven borrower conversion platform that transitions lenders and loan officers from providing advice, not price, to increases in production. www.mortgagecoach.com

Homebot.ai Drives repeat and referral business for real estate agents and mortgage loan officers by helping their clients build wealth. www.homebot.ai

GRAPHIC DESIGN

CANVA OFFERS OVER 50,000 templates for everything from logos, to slide presentations, image templates for Facebook, Instagram, YouTube and more. Each template can be customized with your own text and images using Canva's simple software. www.canva.com

SNAPPA is a web-based graphics editor and alternative to Canva for all kinds of online graphics including social media, blog posts, newsletters, ads, and more! www.snappa.com

REMOVE.BG makes it easy to remove the background from your images (great to isolate a person from a photo to then overlay onto a graphic. www.remove.bg

EASEL is primarily used for creating infographics. You can re-purpose your blog posts into beautiful infographics within minutes. www.easel.ly

OVER Do you ever run into an inspirational quote and want to share it with your audience? You can download app and use your smartphone to customize images by adding colors, text and quotes. You can share these customized images with your audience immediately. Over app available for iOS and Android in app store.

CRM / LEAD MANAGEMENT RESOURCES

LEADPOPS DEVELOPS LEAD generation technology and marketing solutions for mortgage and real estate professionals with a focus on Conversion Rate Optimization. www.leadpops.com

WHITEBOARD Helps mortgage originators create a better a experience with borrowers and partners. Built-in marketing campaigns, templates, phone scripts and more. www.whiteboardcrm.com

BNTOUCH Delivers Automated lead management, branded mobile apps, advanced email marketing & more! Sales Funnels. Share Tasks & Documents. Website Builder. Plug & Play Marketing. www.bntouch.com www.ylopo.com

VERSE.IO (formerly Agentology) is a conversational enablement platform that helps businesses engage, qualify and nurture prospects across multiple channels to drive full-funnel lead conversion. www.verse.io

CALLACTION.IO is an engagement platform captures CALLS, text and email leads to automate lead follow up and nurture with ringless voicemail. www.callaction.co

YLOPO Is a trending real estate website and marketing suite that provides nurturing tools, listing marketing, and sophisticated dynamic Facebook ad management.

REALGEEKS Customer relationship management (CRM) tools make it easier to track and organize leads and existing clients so you can optimize every email and follow-up call. www.realgeeks.com

LIONDESK Is a CRM suite with email automation, task and transaction management, text messaging, power dialing, contact management, conversion tracking, and the ability to record, embed and send videos. www.liondesk.com

PROPERTYBASE Combining a rock solid Salesforce-based CRM with MLS integration, and killer IDX lead-generating websites that work together seamlessly, PropertyBase is a true all-in-one platform that includes drip campaigns, text messaging, a mobile app, call logging, pipelines, a dialer, transaction management and more. www.propertybase.com

CONTACTUALLY is a CRM that gathers all your contacts together, helps you categorize them and understand where they came from, then helps you develop a communication strategy to get them where you want them to go. Contactually integrates with Bold Leads, BombBomb, Facebook, Dotloop, MailChimp, Zillow and more. www.contactually.com

SPACIO allows you to create paperless open house forms to accurately collect visitor information and automatically send follow-up emails after the open house ends. Spacio creates a profile with links to each visitor's social media accounts to help you gain unique insights. www.spacio.com

DOCUSIGN makes it easy to go paperless and get electronic signatures on disclosures, forms, and closing paperwork, regardless of where you—and the buyers and sellers—are. www.docusign.com

HOMESNAP is a free client collaboration app that lets agents and brokers give clients a user-friendly home search experience while obtaining valuable client information. Agents can claim their MLS listing and communicate directly with clients about their favorite properties with in-app messaging. www.homesnap.com

REDX Storm Dialer integrates with your FSBO lists and dials numbers automatically while pulling up pertinent information on your screen. Like everything else in the real estate industry, following up on FSBO and expired listings is a numbers game. The software can also leave a prerecorded voicemail when no one answers. www.theredx.com

SLYBROADCAST skips the phone call and sends thousands of ringless voicemail drop messages directly to your contacts in just minutes. www.slybroadcast.com

FRESHCHAT adds one of the most sticky lead capture options you can have on your website. Live chat! Live chat is the perfect way to capture leads who are leery of phone calls and emails but still want their questions answered ASAP. Freshchat also integrates with Facebook Messenger. www.freshworks.com

DOTLOOP (a Zillow owned company) is an online platform for real estate productivity and transaction optimization. It allows users to collaborate during every stage of a transaction using its form creation, e-signature, and storage capabilities. The platform also has a real-time transaction management system, which includes task templates, automated compliance workflows, and reporting tools. www.dotloop.com

VIDEO RESOURCES

VIDEOLICIOUS MAKES PROFESSIONAL video editing a snap. You can add watermarks, logos, and automatically splice smaller videos into one presentation. Your clients will love the professional-looking videos created. www.videolicious.com

PROMO is like Canva, but for real estate videos. It allows you to easily create real estate videos in minutes using pre-made templates. Simply add your logo, select photos and videos of your listings, change the text and download your video in different sizes for Facebook, Instagram and more.

VIDEOSHOP is one of the best real estate video apps on the market. Packed full features, you can quickly trim and merge clips together, add music, sound effects, text and voice overs as well as apply transitions and filters to personalize your videos.

MAGISTO is much more than a real estate video editing app. It's also a video marketing platform with omni-channel distribution to the likes of Facebook, Instagram, Youtube and Twitter at the touch of a button.

RIPL is great for create eye-catching animated videos for social media. What's more, the Smart Post Recommendations feature provides daily inspiration for what to post next if you're stuck for ideas.

ANIMOTO is easily one of the most popular real estate video apps on this list. The app lets you create high quality, dynamic slideshow videos in a matter of minutes with hundreds of video styles and a growing library of licensed songs.

IMOVIE is Apple's native video editor. You can drag and drop to add clips, then swipe down to split them. Once you've selected your clips, iMovie also offers themes, each with its own set of titles, transitions, and music.

INSHOT is a photo and video editing app especially designed to improve the final result for any video you want to upload to Instagram. This tool includes loads of effects and filters to let you enhance the content you want to share.

BOMBBOMB allows you to engage your audience with videos that are as easy to send as texts and emails, but far more personalized and with much, much higher replies, conversions, and referrals than regular email. www.bombbomb.com

REV Add captions to your videos with 98% accuracy at www.rev.com

SOCIAL MEDIA RESOURCES

PLANOLY IS AN Instagram and Facebook scheduling tool that helps you optimize your social media presence through visual planning and scheduling of content. www.planoly.com

BUFFER If you're a busy agent trying to manage multiple social media accounts, Buffer allows you to pre schedule posts across multiple accounts so you can knock out a few weeks worth of Facebook, Twitter, Linkedin, Instagram and even Pinterest on a few hours on Sunday. www.buffer.com

HOOTSUITE has been around the longest out of any of the scheduling tools. It continues to be one of the most popular social media management tools for posting, scheduling and managing your social media presence. www.hootsuite.com

ALLHASHTAG will help you to create and analyze fast and easy top relevant #HASHTAGS for your social media content and marketing. You can generate thousands of relevant #HASHTAGS that you simply copy and paste into your social media posts to grow your followers. www.all-hashtag.com

BITLY creates trackable URLs, shortens long links and allows you to create your own custom short links for a more professional look when sharing website links. www.bit.ly

VOICE RESOURCES: PODCASTS/ALEXA FLASH BRIEFINGS

THE INDUSTRY SYNDICATE media network includes 30 + different shows across the USA and Canada appealing to any real estate professional, in any segment of the real estate industry. Easily discover, listen to, and connect with the best real estate podcasts, Alexa Flash Briefings, and video shows in the industry. Network and collaborate with other like-minded real estate professionals through the in-app social feed. The first podcast app made specifically for real estate and mortgage pros.

BUZZSPROUT is your simple way to get started with podcasting hosting, syndication, website, tracking listeners and more. They have a simple and user friendly interface ideal for just getting started. www.buzzsprout.com

LIBSYN.COM is the big daddy of podcast hosting, having been around since the early days of podcasting. You can compare it to other platforms at www.libsyn.com

SOUNDUPNOW is your go-to source for all things related to Alexa Flash Briefings. They even host podcasts if you're looking for a single source solution for all your voice needs. www.soundupnow.com

ALEXAFLASHBRIEFINGS Search for Alexa Flash Briefings from around the Universe—also, sign up to have your Flash Briefing included in this directory. www.alexaflashbriefings.com

HEADLINER Want to turn your audio clip into a social media video post with sound and cool looking animated sound waves? Check out www.headliner.app

REV Transcribe your podcast into text for repurposing to blog articles. Add captions to your videos with 98% accuracy at www.rev.com

REPUTATION MANAGEMENT (ONLINE REVIEWS)

SOCIALSURVEY POWERS YOUR online brand to improve your reputation, create social proof and stay compliant. www.socialsurvey.com

TESTIMONIAL TREE Collects your customer's happy stories and turn them into referrals. www.testimonialtree.com

For Additional Resources and Free Book Downloads, Please Visit: www.DisruptOrDieBook.com

SHAMELESS
PLUG

I F YOU'VE GOT this far in the book, my hope is you found it somewhat valuable to your personal success. Today, books are judged by reviews on Amazon. Would it be okay for you to take a few seconds and help us by leaving a review on Amazon?

While I'm asking, it would probably make sense to let you know how else we might be able to help each other.

Being self-published means I can help you directly with bulk orders and save you a fortune. We can also change the cover to match your brokerage or brand and possibly edit some of the featured examples and foreword to deliver a customized version of this book for you.

I would love the opportunity to discuss the opportunity for helping you use this book and accompanying resources to create impact for your clients, employees or partners.

Please email me at: geoff@disruptordiebook.com to learn more about how we can help you build your brand.

ABOUT
THE AUTHOR

GEOFF ZIMPFER IS a former National Sales Trainer with Tony Robbins and has been in the Real Estate and Mortgage industry since 2003. As a successful Mortgage Originator, he consistently closed over 120 loans per year.

As a National Sales Trainer and Coach; Geoff is passionate about bringing real-world strategies and tactics that help Real Estate Agents and Mortgage Loan Originators create engaging, hyper-local personal brands that drive sales and capture consumer direct business. His keynotes and workshops include Personal Branding, Video Marketing, Millennial Marketing, YouTube and the keynote to this book; Disrupt or Die: Surviving the Digital Real Estate Shift.

He is the Founder of the Mortgage Marketing Institute and host of the highly rated podcast; Mortgage Marketing Radio. He's also listed among the Most Connected Mortgage Professionals by National Mortgage Professional Magazine.

WITH GEOFF

www.MortgageMarketingInstitute.com
www.DisruptorDiebook.com
www.MortgageMarketingRadio.com
www.YouTube.com/mortgagemarketinglive

Made in the USA
Columbia, SC
03 November 2021